Peadar O'Donnell
A Reader's Guide

For Kathy, Frankie, and Danielle

Peadar O'Donnell

A Reader's Guide

Alexander G. Gonzalez

Dufour Editions

Published 1997 by Dufour Editions Inc., Chester Springs PA 19425-0007

ISBN 0 8023 1314 0

Library of Congress Cataloging-in-Publication Data:
Gonzalez, Alexander G.
    Peadar O'Donnell: A reader's guide / Alexander Gonzalez.
       p.__cm.
    Includes index.
    ISBN 0-8023-1314-0
    1. O'Donnell, Peadar—Criticism and interpretation —Handbooks,
manuals, etc. 2. Ireland—In literature—Handbooks, manuals, etc.
I. Title.
PR6029.D543Z66   -1997
823'.914—dc20

                                              96-33090
                                              CIP

Printed and bound in Canada

Table Of Contents

Preface

This study was conceived originally as part of a larger research project whose purpose was to study Irish fiction in the age of Joyce. Eventually, however, my focus narrowed until I became preoccupied solely with the novels of Peadar O'Donnell (1893-1986) and eventually with his entire canon, which includes short stories, a play, and three autobiographical books.

I soon noticed how little criticism I could find on O'Donnell — mere mention of his name often serving in place of conscientious literary scrutiny. Literary histories — even as recent as John Wilson Foster's *Fictions of the Irish Literary Revival* (Syracuse University Press, 1987) — tended to ignore O'Donnell for the most part. My curiosity was aroused and the more I read of O'Donnell's work the more I became motivated to undertake a close study of him as a creative artist — rather than as a flamboyant historical figure.

This book — the first of its kind ever attempted on O'Donnell — is intended primarily to be a thorough, comprehensive survey of his literary output: a reader's guide that investigates his canon in considerable detail. Secondarily, it is a contextual book, placing O'Donnell among George Moore, James Joyce, and other modern writers of Irish literature, and ultimately in the larger framework of the modern period in general. Thus far O'Donnell has received a trifling of attention for the realism of his historical novels — such as *Storm* (1925) and *The Knife* (1930) — because they are said to capture "the spirit of the times" of Irish revolution. However, virtually no one has had anything much to say about his less well-known novels, several of which are not mere historical curiosities but fully developed and deeply moving works of art that detail the buoyancy of spirit and hardships of life that coexist in a landscape that is often brutally harsh. Novels such as *Islanders* (1928) — whose title alone suggests a response to Joyce's *Dubliners* – *On the Edge of the Stream* (1934), and *The Big Windows* (1955) will eventually emerge as the foundation of what should be a fine literary reputation. Several other of his novels are flawed but have remarkable points of excellence, and thus also deserve some extended treatment in a full-length study such as this. One example is the naturalistic symbolism in *Adrigoole* (1929).

Grattan Freyer's short monograph, *Peadar O'Donnell* (1973), part of the Bucknell University Press series of the early seventies, was the best available study, but despite some fine insights it is not as useful as one would want, chiefly because of its brevity. It simply attempts to do too much in too little space. His treatment of the major novels is unfortunately very sparse, a problem created in part by the fact that the monograph attempts to be a short biography as well. It is also dated, since Freyer was obviously unable to include any discussion of O'Donnell's final novel, *Proud Island*, which appeared two years after Freyer's study. Michael McInerney's *Peadar O'Donnell, Irish Social Rebel*, is, as its title makes clear, more a biographical than a literary study. Its sole chapter on O'Donnell's creative work is virtually useless to the modern scholar, though McInerney is not to be faulted for this, since this 1974 book is really just an expanded reworking of a series of articles that appeared in *The Irish Times* in 1968; McInerney makes no attempt to pass off the book as a full-blown literary study. The remainder of the work done on O'Donnell is limited to a paragraph or two here and there in a number of surveys and literary histories. Given this paucity of specific commentary on O'Donnell's work, the need for a study such as this became manifestly clear.

Finally, I would like to thank those who have aided me at various stages in the development of this book. Peadar O'Donnell, Jr., generously granted me permission to quote from his father's works. Joseph Hynes, John Sherwood, Don Taylor, Kathleen Dubs, Martin Jacobi, Matthew C. Roudane, and Edmund Epstein all receive my gratitude for their advice in the earliest stages of composition. I am also indebted to Morris Beja, John and Betty Messenger, Richard Finneran, and Barton R. Friedman for reading portions of the manuscript and offering their expert advice.

And I am grateful to Robert Hogan for granting me permission to reprint some of my work on O'Donnell's stories and on *The Big Windows* that originally appeared in the *Journal of Irish Literature*.

I would also like to thank those who have aided me here at Cortland College of the State University of New York. Robert Rhodes has always been patient and kind in dealing with me. Immensely beneficial in the book's development was release time provided by the Department of English under a program developed by the former Chair, Del Ivan Janik. Also of tremendous support was a grant from the Faculty Research Program, funded by the Research Foundation of the State University of New York and awarded by the College Research Committee, chaired by Charles Spink. This grant was especially helpful since it was provided to me in the early stages of writing when such a timely award gave me immeasurable encouragement to proceed. I am further indebted to Martha Atkins, who helped me develop a strong proposal. I would also like to express my gratitude to Susan Stout and Marilyn Bradley, whose patience in dealing with me while typing the manuscript was absolutely commendable. Lastly, I would like to thank my family and friends, all of whom bore with me until this project reached fruition. I owe a significant debt to all.

Establishing a Literary-Historical Context

That fiction is "the weak point of the [Irish] Revival"[1] is a view long-held by literary critics. Indeed, Ernest Boyd's pronouncement was echoed about thirty years later by Benedict Kiely, who affirmed that this celebrated period in Irish letters was "mainly a matter for poets and playwrights."[2] Later on, Richard Fallis noted that "fiction developed most slowly of all the genres in the Irish Renaissance."[3] And, most recently, William J. McCormack cites "the Renaissance's . . . coolness towards the novel."[4] The important question raised by such statements is whether the fiction was deemed inferior merely relative to poetry and drama or, in a more general sense, simply inferior once we go beyond James Joyce and George Moore, the strength of whose fiction is recognized by virtually all critics of the Renaissance years. The brilliance of these two writers, when added to that of W. B. Yeats, J. M. Synge, and Sean O'Casey, cast a long shadow over the work of other able authors, especially writers of fiction such as Liam O'Flaherty and James Stephens, whose work has come under close scrutiny only relatively recently.[5] But beyond O'Flaherty and Stephens are a number of "lesser authors" who produced valuable work, much of which has hardly been studied with any care and some of which has essentially never been evaluated .

One of the principal authors relegated to this third tier is Peadar O'Donnell, who began writing in the twenties and went on to produce seven novels, a play, and three autobiographical books. Unfairly ignored, O'Donnell seems to me one of several victims of a literary period that produced so many writers of superior merit that authors such as O'Donnell have stood little chance of attaining any real recognition. Some of O'Donnell's writing is, in fact, of the highest order, even if his entire canon — which is of uneven quality — precludes his being ranked alongside Joyce and the several other acknowledged greats. O'Donnell deserves to be recognized not only for the excellence of parts of his canon but for literary-historical reasons as well. Several English authors of no greater merit, such as Gissing and Galsworthy, are much better known and have been accorded a far more prominent place in the literary history of their native country.

Also working against O'Donnell is the innate prejudice demonstrated by the majority of literary critics toward writers of Renaissance rural Irish fiction, and O'Donnell seems to me one of the chief victims of Joyce's urban legacy. It might, of course, be argued that in works such as *The Untilled Field* (1903), Moore wrote perfectly respectable rural fiction, but his perspective is not one of a rural writer who has experienced rural life day in and day out. Rather, we sense a writer fairly detached from his subject matter, as if his characters were more a kind of cute literary curiosity than fully realistic and well fleshed-out creations. Moore's anticlerical thesis further serves to narrow his focus, so that the flavor of rural life is at best only partially rendered.

Yet O'Donnell does nevertheless share significant traits with both Joyce and Moore, such as his interest in physical paralysis as metaphor for spiritual stasis. A novel that has essentially never before been fully evaluated, *On the Edge of the Stream* (1934), minutely details the steady exhaustion of its would-be adulterous heroine, Nelly McFadden Joyce. In the same novel, O'Donnell experiments meaningfully with narrated interior monologue, which occurs in forceful, sporadic bursts that serve well to humanize his serious characters and give them added relief from the cartoon-like humorous ones in this brilliant, problematic novel whose seriocomic contrapuntal structure is perhaps the main reason critics have tended to shy away from it.

When we consider O'Donnell's connection to Moore, it is well worth looking beyond *The Untilled Field* and *The Lake* (1905)to Moore's most famous novel, *Esther Waters* (1894), which O'Donnell is highly likely to have read as a young man. This essentially Irish story[6] broadly affected much Renaissance fiction, despite its English characters and setting. In its first edition, Moore declared the struggles of his endearingly laudable protagonist to be "an heroic adventure: a mother's fight . . . against all the forces that civilisation arrays against the lowly."[7] If Esther is in this modern sense heroic, then it seems to me that the determination to survive exhibited by some of O'Donnell's characters, perhaps most notably Mary Doogan, in *Islanders*, qualifies them for the same status, even if the settings are exclusively rural. The brutal Irish countryside can marshal some formidable forces of its own — such as famine, the allotment of poor rocky land, cruel landlords, and a generally oppressive economic and political system. Some of O'Donnell's characters can well envision a more materially successful life abroad, but are unwilling to leave behind their families and tightly knit communal way of life. Just as Esther Waters resists the repeated temptations of abandoning her baby, O'Donnell's protagonists stoically resist the temptation of abandoning their centuries-old traditional way of life. O'Donnell's Mary Doogan is heroic in the same ways, but, simply because she is an admirable woman who eventually starves to death, as Esther is also clearly willing to do, in order to keep her children fed, the connection to *Esther Waters* may be even stronger. Anyone who has read Moore's novel can hardly read *Islanders* without instantly making the association — despite the fact that O'Donnell's novel is set in rural Ireland. Moore's "Derby Day" scenes are even echoed in *Islanders*, albeit on a reduced scale.

Some of Moore's work after *The Untilled Field* is also highly influential. The "melodic line," a flowing effect Moore sought to cultivate in his prose toward the later stages of his career, is imitated by O'Donnell in his best novel, *The Big Windows* (1955). Also, Moore's symbolist novel, *The Lake*, has had a far-reaching effect on several novels written soon afterward, perhaps most famously on Brinsley MacNamara's *The Valley of the Squinting Windows* (1918), but also on O'Donnell's *Adrigoole* (1929). The symbolic value of the lake in Moore's novel is adapted by O'Donnell to fit his most pessimistic book: where Father Gogarty can swim across his lake to spiritual emancipation, Hughie Dalach is mired in bogland from which he cannot extricate himself and in which, in a spiritual sense, he drowns.

But O'Donnell is most original and insightful when he presents — with great sympathy — the hard life led in rural Ireland by those who did not seek exile and chose instead to remain in their native country and tough it out. Thus do Donegal's people and their problems come to life, and the result is often deeply moving. Their loneliness and isolation, their anomie in the face of sweeping social and political changes, are sensitively handled and investigated; for some, the sense of disconnection brought grotesque psychological problems and strange fixations as they attempted to adjust to the new Ireland. Such anomie is strongly manifested in the work of O'Donnell, who offers us a veritably photographic realism in depicting both island life, in *Islanders*, and glen life, in *The Big Windows*. Like Daniel Corkery and Seumas O'Kelly, O'Donnell excels in rendering a strong sense of community in rural villages. And he does not conveniently veer away from its unpleasant facets — the grubbiness of the new materialism and the acquisitiveness of the long-downtrodden peasant farmer.

But this is not to say that his literary works are relentlessly gloomy, even if a significant portion is written in the naturalistic vein. O'Donnell also shows us the simple joys of rural life, reveals the sustaining, underlying sense of everyday happiness that buoys the rural Irishman in even the worst of times. Overall there emerges a level of human dignity that we would in all likelihood miss or not fully appreciate without the work done by O'Donnell, for in minutely limning the privations that were suffered, he presents a fuller picture than it is possible to gather from the work of the other playwrights and novelists of the time, who usually had loftier, abstract, and more universal considerations in mind.

Introduction and Biographical Sketch

Peadar O'Donnell was born in 1893 in his beloved Donegal, where he eventually became a local schoolmaster, both on the mainland and on Aranmore, a large coastal island that was the site of his first writing efforts. During this period of his life he developed an interest in socialist thought, especially following a highly influential trip to Scotland. By 1919 O'Donnell's allegiance to the Republican cause was secure, and he was clearly committed to the idea that force was necessary to free Ireland. A good deal can be said about O'Donnell's political career — complete with arrests, jailings, escapes, and wounds — but much has already been written about this aspect of his life.[8] Indeed, the biographical material I provide makes no attempt to appear complete; I offer only such information as seems relevant to his creative output, a substantial portion of which is clearly autobiographical. Suffice it to say that throughout his life he was a champion of the political left, not only in opposing the British but also in forcefully resisting what he saw as the compromises of the Free State. A supporter of socialist causes in the social as well as political realm, he believed in the establishment of cooperative stores as one way of checking the rampant gombeenism ushered in during the grab-bag early days of the Free State, and he opposed the use of religion as a platform for right-wing politics. I would not call O'Donnell properly "anticlerical," as some critics do, because the fact is that most of the clergy did take sides in the Anglo-Irish war, and his political differences with such a group must perforce appear anticlerical — but is it possible to criticize the clergy on political grounds without seeming to be anticlerical? As Daniel Corkery does, in *The Hounds of Banba* (1920),

O'Donnell takes the clergy to task *only* as citizens who are not doing their duty to their country; in no sense is O'Donnell anticlerical in the way George Moore, for instance, can be, because, again like Corkery, O'Donnell has no problem with priests who confine their fervor to their religion without overtly taking sides against those fighting for Ireland's freedom. After an irreconcilable break with De Valera in 1932, O'Donnell went on to abandon his connection with the IRA, and thus ended his direct involvement in Irish politics. His association with *The Bell*, both as "managing editor" under Sean O'Faolain until 1946 and as editor proper until 1954, is well documented.[9] His three autobiographical tomes, *The Gates Flew Open* (1932), *Salud!* (1936), and *There Will Be Another Day* (1963), have received some attention, but his work as novelist and playwright, however, continues to be the most neglected portion of his major contributions to Irish culture.

Relative to the work of other writers of rural fiction — such as Corkery, Seumas O'Kelly, Brinsley MacNamara, and Darrell Figgis — O'Donnell's is by far the least complicated. Both thematically and structurally, his work is, in fact, simple; his strength as a writer lies in that very simplicity, which, in his best work, allows for a richer texture — a full, at times almost photographic, rendering of peasant life. With plot machinations at an absolute minimum, he instead relies on the intensity of the simple scenes he presents — a method that yields a greater intimacy than we see in the work of these other rural writers, including Darrell Figgis's *Children of Earth* (1918), which is perhaps the most detailed and lovingly written portrait of island life to appear prior to O'Donnell's novels. The love affairs in O'Donnell's novels are mundane, even pedestrian, compared to that between Figgis's Eoghan O'Clery and Nancy Flaherty, but the wonder of love, its ability to transform and nurture individuals, is unobtrusively heightened in O'Donnell's best literary works. Indeed, the canvas of day-to-day life is effectively complete, so that what love actually means on an everyday level is well brought out in his portraits of the remote townlands and islands of Donegal.

In fact, that remoteness is of vital importance to O'Donnell, who is concerned with the unpolluted rural Irish community, and this is reflected in the pattern of location found in his novels: *Storm* (1925) and *Islanders* (1928) take place on Donegal islands, but since early in this century the Donegal coast remained essentially as remote, O'Donnell began to move his settings inland; *Adrigoole* (1929) is about a coastal townland, *The Knife* (1930) takes us right into the Lagan Valley, and *On the Edge of the Stream* (1934) is set far enough inland that the Lagan is not even mentioned; however, by this time O'Donnell could see the inroads being made by modern civilization, so in *The Big Windows* (1955), which is set in the same townland of his previous novel, he explores the social changes that are occurring by sending into it a strong-tempered island woman whose open-mindedness makes her in many ways superior to the glen dwellers; and finally, in *Proud Island* (1975), O'Donnell returns completely to his original focus — life on a tiny island. The circularity of this pattern reflects both O'Donnell's attempts to broaden his scope and his eventual realization that he is most effective when he writes about places where unbridled natural forces often erupt to alter the lives of men — and where political concerns are relatively unimportant.

Storm

O'Donnell's first novel, *Storm*, probably appeared in 1925, although the first edition is not dated and may have been issued early in 1926. Grattan Freyer reports that O'Donnell wrote it partly in jail and partly after his escape, a disjointed process that no doubt is partially responsible for the novel's uneven quality.[10] Vivian Mercier calls it "a beginner's effort," no more than "a series of sketches of island life and the Anglo-Irish War,"[11] and Freyer's rightly restrained response is to acknowledge its "unadorned simplicity."[12] The novel's early pages are its best as it focuses on the island of Arranmore, the storm that erupts one day, and the heroic nature of Eamonn Gallagher, the central character. Once the novel's emphasis shifts toward the military and political concerns of the Anglo-Irish war, however, its vitality and cohesiveness are greatly diminished and the generally weak characterization disintegrates almost completely.

As Freyer has observed, the "storm" of the title is a "double symbol" — not only the actual physical storm that struck the northern Irish coast in 1919, but also the political upheaval that followed.[13] The novel's very first pages, a depiction of nature's fury suddenly arising, are evidence of a finely honed realism. Three homely images — of buckets clattering down the street, of creels tumbling over, and of sand grains "pelting against the window" — provide a dual function: first they realistically draw us into the scene, and then, immediately after, through a sort of spontaneous, communal sympathetic imagination, serve to trigger a picture that flashes across the minds of the island's inhabitants — a picture of "living fishermen fighting, struggling" out in their boats.[14] The storm's animistic presentation adds to the feeling of malevolent forces at work, as when the "darkening sky scowls on the water, [and] white-tipped crests hiss and snarl, smashing their faces against the bows, gurning and spitting along the sides" (20-21). Such a technique suggests Figgis's *Children of Earth*, published eight or nine years earlier, especially since both novels open with storm scenes as viewed from tiny Western islands, but where O'Donnell's storm is, I think, to be taken as a naturalistic force, Figgis makes sure we see it as disinterested —unconcerned with the lives of men. An effective structural device amplifies O'Donnell's opening: the second chapter takes us out to the one boat that is unable to make it in with the others and shows the storm's arrival from the point of view of its occupants as well. This dual presentation serves to emphasize Eamonn's heroism for taking the lifeboat out to effect such a daring rescue, for this is clearly no ordinary storm, and the realism of the sailors' terror complements the abstract inklings of the worried islanders.

There can be no doubt that O'Donnell intends for Eamonn to be a heroic figure, first with the rescue of the otherwise doomed fishermen and later as a rebel fighting against the British. This reform-minded schoolteacher-turned-revolutionary is obviously based on a part of O'Donnell himself, who underwent similar experiences during the same turbulent times. Like his creator, Eamonn is intolerant of clerical interference but is not otherwise anticlerical; to counterbalance a meddlesome local priest, Father Willie, who denounces Eamonn from the altar, O'Donnell gives us Father McAllister, who becomes a friend of Eamonn's family and keeps his religious duties and his political views separate. Eamonn's consciousness is very thinly presented for the most part, but O'Donnell does a particularly good job once Eamonn is shot and tries to elude his captors. The impressions recorded in the wounded man's mind are kaleidoscopic and shockingly random — "the hysterical cry of a child," some cows "racing up and down the plain," the irregular feel of the ground under his feet, the hissing sound made by a bullet, the terrible thirst he develops, and his struggle not to faint (118-19). It is unfortunate, however, that these gripping passages are subsequently undercut just two pages later by blatant political propaganda with socialist leanings (121); rather than sounding like the thoughts of a wounded rebel concerned with his own life and the struggle immediately at hand, they are abstract, "lofty" considerations about Ireland's future — inappropriate for their context. This lapse into propaganda is thankfully only temporary — Eamonn's last words, for example, return us to the realism typical of the novel's best parts: his patriotic thoughts are not abstract but specifically and genuinely concerned with arrangements to be made for his wake — at which he pleads that no rebels be present because the risk of capture is too great.

Eamonn's lack of selfish concerns is an indicator of the value his author places on the sense of community, both local and national. We have already seen the communal imagination sympathetically engaged when the storm strikes the fishermen, and if the islanders initially look upon the rebels with suspicion, then we must recall how uncomfortable they feel about *any* breaks with custom and tradition, even in such things as the "certain order of arrangement" for seats at village meetings (32). But the tremendous sense of community usually associated with island life eventually reveals itself, not only in the support given to men on the run, but also in the comfort and care so often accorded those men.

The novel's best realistic scenes point to its limited strengths. On several occasions, for instance, O'Donnell shows his extensive knowledge of arms, knowledge so detailed that we cannot doubt its autobiographical origins. On the other hand, the novel's limitations are more numerous and more severe, the most damaging being the long stretches that read like propagandistic pulp fiction — as when O'Donnell describes a raid on a police barracks, which is captured: the rebels' gallantry is accented while the loss of life is barely mentioned and thereby effectively de-emphasized (93-103). Still, even if *Storm* cannot be called a good novel, it is not at all bad for a first effort written under duress. It has a few excellent scenes and serves as a preliminary for the emergence of O'Donnell's best material, which was soon to follow.

Islanders

Islanders, published in America as *The Way It Was with Them*, is the most moving of O'Donnell's early novels. In 1943, Vivian Mercier called it "The most successful . . . of O'Donnell's books, a faithful, absolutely unforced account of island life" that gives "an un-heightened . . . sense of everyday" existence.[15] All critics since Mercier's original appraisal have hailed the novel's quiet power, perhaps most recently Johann Norstedt, who in 1983 called it "a gripping story" that reflects O'Donnell at his best.[16] Clearly the passing of sixty years since its original appearance has not lessened the novel's appeal — which is broad enough to attract not only those who love literature, but anthropologists, folklorists, and so-ciologists as well. Freyer notes that *Islanders* was conceived and written in prison and then smuggled out by a friendly jailer.[17]

The islanders' hand-to-mouth existence is so realistically por-trayed that we are brought into scene after scene as if we were actu-ally observing each one directly for ourselves. One extended series of scenes, before, during, and after the regatta, is a qualitative counterpart to George Moore's famous Derby Day scenes in *Esther Waters* (1894), only O'Donnell's canvas is considerably smaller and more restrained. O'Donnell is certainly no less frank when he shows us the betting, the cheering throng, the splurging after vic-tory (a shilling for a cup of tea), the procession of drunkards, and the spectacle of relatively gauche islanders let loose among people with finer tastes and more refined social norms. Mary Doogan's references to horse racing further serve to suggest Moore's novel as we read along.[18]

The sense of family—resilient, supportive, loving —is at the heart of this basically naturalistic novel. Mary Doogan, the family's spiritual anchor through most of the novel, is stoically heroic in the same self-denying manner of Daniel Corkery's heroes or Moore's Esther Waters. Through her own slow starvation Mary is better able to feed her children and keep the family strong. And we are given enough evidence to deduce that O'Donnell's novel is about a *people*, of which this family is for the most part merely representative. For instance, during the first fifth of the novel, reference is made to Mary by her position in the family — "the mother" — instead of by her name, a method that draws attention to the precariousness of that role in this naturalistic setting. O'Donnell is even more overt, however, when he has the doctor tell us that he comes "across it again and again . . . just hunger, not a thing else . . . always the mother" who dies (37; ellipses are O'Donnell's). Even on her death bed, Mary's concerns are still caught up in the flow of family life, in the act of survival: she worries if anyone has brought in the eggs before Neddy's dog can get them, if the ducks are "at the hens' mate" (207), that the black cow not "get a shower of rain," and that the calf must be given its drink of water (208). Psychologically entangled in the performance of her last domestic acts, she is caught in an elongated moment of time — permanently trapped in the middle of her tasks. Life has pummelled her with uncountable blows until, worn out, she has finally stumbled. The starkness of island life — and of this entire novel — is brought home by the small detail that closes the chapter on Mary's death: a book must be placed beneath her chin in order to keep her lifeless mouth from falling open (210).

Charlie Doogan, her son, is also of heroic stature before the onslaught of naturalistic forces, only he is heroic in the more conventional sense: he possesses great physical strength, fortitude, and courage. On an everyday level, he strives hard to ward off family hunger by relentlessly fishing, "slaving at the work, but there are few results, beyond occasional exhaustion" (69). In extraordinary situations, Charlie's heroism is more obvious: when a difficult pregnancy and a storm conspire and threaten to take his sister Peggy's life, Charlie attempts to launch a boat so he can bring the doctor from the mainland, but when those efforts fail because of the exceptionally rough seas, he puts his life into greater jeopardy by using a curragh instead — actions that put us in mind of the undaunted Eoghan O'Clery in *Children of Earth*. In fact, Charlie cuts almost as romantic a figure as Eoghan when he arrives at the doctor's half-drowned — romantic enough to sweep Ruth, the doctor's sister, off her feet. His stature in her eyes grows considerably after he saves her from drowning (129-30) and after he is victorious in the regatta, which he earlier promises to win in her honor.

O'Donnell is effective in realistically demonstrating the naturalistic pattern that is not relentlessly negative. Like Zola's, O'Donnell's naturalism includes positive surges, as when a rich shoal of herring uplifts the local economy and brings relative prosperity to the suffering islanders. But not long after, two of Charlie's sisters must be hired out on the mainland — a fairly standard income-producing practice — and the strain on the family is severe: as Mary puts it, "it's hard to send soft childer[sic] out to work among the stranger" (75), and previously she has wondered if the family will ever be together again as a whole unit (62) — a foreshadowing of Nellie's death, from a neglected appendicitis, which she suffers alone, in pain, for days in a barn loft (86). During this period their cow dies (65), and then their hens (89). Nellie's death, however, is not only an emotional loss, but also an added financial hardship: for her wake, they must sell their new cow. Thus is Charlie, in turn, forced first into poaching and later into stealing a sack of flour (209), which he does, however, eventually replace. Interspersed among these disheartening events is a constant sense of family joy on an everyday level. A good example of one of O'Donnell's warm domestic scenes comes in the twenty-first chapter, when Sheila, Charlie's little sister, creeps into bed with him, brings him back his breakfast, and then shares it with him (105-06). Unfortunately, later on, Sally, the older sister who cooked the breakfast, finds herself in a major downswing upon her mother's death: like many of Brinsley MacNamara's pathetic unmarried individuals, Sally is fated to remain a spinster until all the family's children are grown and gone — but by then she will be too old and worn out to attract a husband.

One more naturalistic force yet remains to be discussed: the chemical power of sexual attraction. Actually, O'Donnell allies such an attraction with romance, as opposed to clear-sighted realism. Charlie is in fact torn between Ruth, who represents the former quality, and Susan Manus, who represents the latter. Charlie does not feel "the strong call of the mating instinct" (70) for Susan, who, like him, is an islander, a known quantity; rather, he is helplessly haunted by the face of the exotic, ethereal Ruth (180-81), even when he tries not to think of her. Neither does Susan feel any overpowering attraction to Charlie, who does not excite her the way Sean Friel, a romantic rebel from the mainland, clearly does. But after Friel eventually rejects Susan and Charlie communes with himself over what is wisest for his future, the two make the sensible choice: they will marry after all, once they have learned through their trials with outsiders that grand passions must yield before an everyday suitability, a rightness that will be enhanced by their life together on Inniscara. O'Donnell does make a sociological issue out of these relationships. For instance, Ruth does not truly see how difficult life is on the island; she instead maintains a romantic, Yeatsian view of such a life among charming but rough-mannered peasants. Similarly, Charlie feels ill at ease away from his island and realistically decides he would be happier to stay at home. Such is not the case, however, with all islanders, who are themselves torn, some seeing island life as healthful and wholesome and others seeing their existence only as relentlessly hand-to-mouth (134-41), a life from which to escape if the means can be found. Indeed, the exile theme is fairly strong, as both Charlie and Susan have contemplated emigration (70, 72), and much is made of the money sent back by dutiful children gone to America. These last few concerns form a substantial part of *Proud Island*, a novel written by O'Donnell nearly fifty years later.

But overall, the sense of a tight-knit community is strong — as if it were an extension of the family, able to sustain its individual members no matter what might befall any of them. Sometimes the community helps its members in simple ways, as when Charlie helps his neighbor, Neil Rodgers, to thatch his roof — and O'Donnell draws no special attention to this fact; instead, we see it as an unthinking, normal part of island life. Of course, the greater the distress, the greater the communal response, as with Nellie's death. O'Donnell often gives us whole chapters of dialogue (*e.g.*, 147-52) that offer close glimpses into the peasant psyche, an effect again familiar from Figgis's *Children of Earth*, only in O'Donnell's novel such dialogue is more truly communal than limited to family discussion. Community values are thus exposed, as when a substantial amount of money is paid to the priest unresentfully, just as any other expense would be (74). Other insights into the peasant consciousness appear as narrated interior monologue, such as Charlie's self-communion while rowing toward the main island (179-81). Through these various methods, O'Donnell gives us a remarkably clear and unheightened picture of life and love on a Donegal island. His next four novels will attempt to do the same for mainland communities.

Adrigoole

Adrigoole is the novel of O'Donnell's that is most conventionally naturalistic. Where *Islanders* ends with a relative upswing in the central characters' fortunes — Charlie and Susan are to be married — *Adrigoole* is more relentless and considerably more gloomy in depicting good people caught up in a swirl of forces that are beyond their control and often beyond their understanding. For these reasons, both Freyer and Jeffares have used the term "tragic" in describing *Adrigoole*, which is certainly as tragic and depressing as Dreiser's *An American Tragedy* (1925), for example, although not as thoroughly documented.[19,20] O'Donnell wrote the novel in Dublin, a considerably more relaxed creative environment than that in which he wrote his first two novels.[21] One must wonder whether this circumstance was not in some ways unfortunate from a literary standpoint, for Mercier has quite rightly noted that, relative to the novels preceding it, *Adrigoole* is a "pretentious . . . more self-conscious work of art."[22] That self consciousness, however, is not always a flaw, but it does make for an uneven work that starts out as a painstakingly limned *bildungsroman* and eventually, as the author appears to lose patience with his material, degenerates into a rough tumble into the naturalistic abyss.

The opening backdrop is impressive. Mountains, "sombre, muscular, massive, full-breasted with earthliness,"[23] loom over the townland much as Figgis's gods and goddesses frame the island setting of *Children of Earth*. In the foreground, O'Donnell takes us through a rapid survey of farmers' activities during each of the four seasons; and finally we reach the level of the soil itself — including the energy-sucking bog and the "roots of heather that push downward; eating downward, waiting for the men below to weaken; waiting to go back without feeling" (5). Such statements establish the naturalistic frame of perception and act to cast a kind of pall over the whole book.

As has been mentioned, the novel begins as a *bildungsroman*. Immediately after O'Donnell has finished establishing the setting, we are introduced to twelve-year-old Hughie Dalach, in school, impressing the school inspector with his knowledge and shrewdness. Clearly, he is the best-equipped of O'Donnell's early protagonists to face the naturalistic universe. This school scene, wherein we meet the memorable Tommy Not' in' and Danny Rogers, is delightful — one of the most effective in the novel. Other good scenes follow, such as that in the third chapter, where old Hughie watches over his son, Cormac, who is digging a drainage ditch and who is later joined by his own son, young Hughie Dalach; there is far more than sentimental value in the image of the three generations thus congregated, for the consciousness of each one is so rendered as to create a network of nuances, both straightforward and ironic, before the grey naturalistic background. Also worthy is the scene where Hughie sees his grandfather for the last time before going away to the Lagan for the hiring fair (24). Hughie's voyage has many memorable scenes in which he learns about life beyond his townland, and eventually eight years pass while he is hired out, during which time he dutifully sends money home. When he returns to the Rosses, already a man, he is disappointed, for the local country now seems poor and the living scant compared to what he has grown accustomed to in the Lagan (77-8), but its people soon warm his heart enough to the point where he is glad to be back. He now, however, possesses the needed perspective to realize occasionally just how marginal existence can be in his poor townland. The final important scene in this first section of the novel is Hughie's first sight, from a mountain top, of Adrigoole — a lush townland of rich soil, high up in a glen (88). Eventually, Hughie will be enabled to live there when, after he marries Brigid, her old uncle, Neddie, gives them his farm. It should be added that throughout these early pages O'Donnell reminds us that there are many "Hughies," not just the one with whom his story is concerned.

Even the final stages of Hughie's stay in the Lagan are glossed over and presented only in the most general terms — a sign of the novel's eventual breakdown after its strong opening. The *bildungsroman* part is framed by naturalistic elements that occur in two distinct sections: one is comprised of the very first few pages and the second does not appear until almost a hundred and fifty pages later. Besides the backdrop already discussed, this suggestive first section also makes strong hints about how the bogland absorbs human effort the same way it absorbs water and about the precariousness of existence: naturalistic details are effectively presented, as when a sleeping child grinds his teeth and his parents must immediately worry because "maybe there's worms in him" (28). Some of these chapters, such as the second and fourth, end with a naturalistic epilogue of sorts: an all but thematically disconnected accounting of physical facts that place the novel's central occurrences in a larger context —with the sense of ongoing life: "In a beam of sunlight from the small window, dust glinted and danced, a mouse rustled in the grate; the children, packed tight together in the desks, listened with open mouths and breathed out and in together; outside a man whistled sharply for a dog"(12).

The telling of these events serves no purpose other than to relate whatever has just happened to the greater flow of life. On the other hand, O'Donnell is sometimes less subtle, as in the embedded story of Hughie the Mason, a strong farmer who is "bull-necked, short-backed, [and] boxed shouldered [sic]" : after years of toil, he is no more than "a beaten man, with heather sprouting on his doorstep and his body clogged with asthma" (13). Some readers may at this point remember Edward Martyn's Carden Tyrrell, who, in *The Heather Field* (1899), suffers a similar fate.

The second naturalistic section, which mostly shows Hughie and Brigid's fortunes spiraling downward, is far longer and more conventional. The plot becomes melodramatic, as Richard Fallis has observed,[24] and its pace, not surprisingly, accelerates — losing much of the opening's leisurely detailed, photographic qualities. From the apex of their fortunes — with the couple married and living on Neddie's farm amid times of plenty (240) — we witness their steady decline: rebel soldiers who are harbored deplete the farm's resources; rain and floods set back Hughie's farming; a blight wipes out the potatoes; the family falls heavily into debt trying to make up for its patriotic generosity; and because they are overextended, everything the family tries seems to fail. Then the civil war erupts and Hughie and Neddy are shot; Neddie dies, but Hughie manages a partial recovery from his leg wound (265). The gloomy trend continues: doctor bills mount up, Republican soldiers keep staying with the family, the fields stand in need of ploughing, and rent arrears are sought (269, 272). But Hughie still manages to struggle vigorously and, to bring in needed money, even goes to work in Scotland — where he is struck down by typhoid fever, from which he never totally recovers. After another start in Ireland, in spite of such failures, he returns to Scotland, and for a while things seem to improve, but the death of his daughter, Grania — from eating hemlock the hungry child mistook for wild carrot (286) — signals the onset of the final descent. Crops are bad, Hughie's wound develops sores and, driven to find some means of making quick money, Hughie is caught making illegal alcohol (294). Sentenced to a year in jail, Hughie is released after serving seven months, but he arrives home only to find that Brigid, the baby, and one other child have died — all from hunger (326-27). When the novel closes, Hughie, a broken man, is taken to the asylum.

Though most of the emphasis in the last half of the novel falls upon Hughie, Brigid is accorded her share of individual attention: her own phrase for her perception of how life treats her is "the world has its hoof on me" (196). Brigid especially feels this way when Mickey Sheila is frequently wooing her; she "might as well do what the rabbit does when a weasel gets after it — lie down on its back and wait for him" (171). The image is successful not only because of its sexual suggestion but also because of its predatory nature, for Brigid really does feel hunted. But is Hughie not pursuing her as well? The difference is that she feels no innate, chemical attraction for Mickey, whom she sees as a "dead old man" (168) who makes her feel "ashamed" (167); Hughie, on the other hand, is young, handsome, strong (168), and produces "less a thought than a feeling" so that "her blood ran warmly," and "colour crept into her cheeks" (186) just at the sight of him. Of course, to these overwhelming feelings she can offer no resistance.

Finally, we should pay some attention to the naturalistic role of the malevolent bog that lurks at the edge of the outer fields and beneath the soil itself. Like the Dutch reclaiming land from the sea, the people of this glen drain off water in reclaiming land from the bog. As Hughie puts it: "it's hard to drive bog deep, an' it sucks an' sucks at any life above it" (251). While in prison he worries primarily about the advances the bog may be making in his absence, for "without help [Brigid] would be drowned in bog" (315), and he even has nightmares about it: he sees his house on fire but as he fights his way inside all that his "clawing hands" can grip is "clammy bog" that makes his fingers turn numb (319). And when Hughie begins to rely on the repeated phrase, "God would make things right" (311), we soon see that such is not the case at all: that god is like an *ignis fatuus* in the bog — false light, false hope. The bog is in many ways the equivalent of what the lake is in Moore's novel, *The Lake* . It becomes the central symbol, not only of the protagonist's spiritual fortunes, but also of Ireland itself. Just as Father Gogarty finds on the lake a wounded curlew, whose legs have been tied together, that symbolizes his own spiritual paralysis, so does Hughie find in the swampland a frog that, with a broken leg, is struggling toward the nearby lake — and in the frog's plight he sees symbolized his own weakened condition, especially if we recall that he himself has only recently been shot in the leg (281). Gogarty swims the lake and escapes spiritual death in Ireland, but Hughie cannot extricate himself from the bog that holds him fixed, and he is eventually all but swallowed up by the wet earth of his native country. The idea of the frog also suggests Moore's story, "The Wild Goose," in one scene of which Ned Carmady, the protagonist, watches a snake sucking down a frog that delays too long before trying to escape the snake's jaws; in this metaphor, the snake represents Ireland and the frog any Irishman who delays too long before going into exile. Since Hughie and Brigid have both strongly considered exile, the connection is firm enough: Ireland absorbs all the energy expended by its people and then eventually devours them, even as bogland eventually gobbles up the farmland that people have reclaimed from it. Given that this is by far the most pessimistic of O'Donnell's novels, such readings are invited by the mere tenor of the book. I would even go so far as to suggest that the now-selfconscious O'Donnell was more intent on writing a characteristically naturalistic novel than on expressing ideas and emotions he felt to be consistently true about his native country. Indeed, O'Donnell once indicated some regret about the novel's gloomy ending, wishing he would have had Hughie emigrate instead.[25] Judging by the relative optimism of the rest of his fiction, it is even easier to see *Adrigoole* as a quirk —perhaps merely reflecting the author's temporary pessimism during some low point in his personal life or overall view of life.

As usual, however, the novel offers us a close, warm view of communal life with its unusual habits, customs, and mores. When a bullock breaks its leg and must be killed, the custom is "to play cards on him" so that none of the animal will go to waste; good-luck items utilized by a player include holy water, a live cricket, and the act of having the tongs thrown after him by a man (166). Time is told not by clocks or watches but by other signs: when Hughie needs to be woken up early one morning, the time will be right "when the cluster of stars is over Brennan's" (27). And by watching the smoke rise from neighbors' chimneys, a person can tell "the order in which [they] had stirred" (99). Interestingly, the townland's most prominently described mores all have a negative aspect to them of some sort. When Brigid's uncle Neddie walks her home one night — thereby thwarting the wooing Mickey Sheila — Neddie's actions are interpreted as "hostility to Mickey" (145). On the road to the Lagan, we see the humiliation suffered by poor children who have to eat "Indian bread" instead of real bread; and when Hughie realizes that Brigid's lunch is not the equal of his own, he is socially tactful and sits far enough away not to "see" what she is eating (33-5). The episode is sociologically interesting because it reveals how stratified this society can be when food is at issue, even determining how close people can sit to one another and what airs the children can assume relative to the quality of their food. And the deeply ingrained work ethic, seen primarily in the hard labor put into the fields, is underscored when Hughie is in jail: in the same spirit as his farmwork is performed, Hughie scours out the cracks between the floorboards of his cell even as he once dug drains in his fields. It is compulsive behavior that, however, helps him maintain his sanity. Finally, it is worth mentioning the interesting eighteenth chapter, in which we see a commendably realistic detailing of a typical night indoors among neighbors: we feel as if we are in the same room with these people. But if this community is so close-knit, then why does it permit Brigid and her children to die from hunger? It would appear the community has failed here until we are told that the Dalach house has remained isolated ever since Hughie's bout with typhoid fever — which all the neighbors regretfully fear to contract (328), even more than a year after Hughie's "recovery." James Cahalan, however, ascribes her ostracism to the fact that her Republican husband has been imprisoned.[26]

The community's gossip receives some attention, but it is quite a contrast to the bitter portrait rendered in Brinsley MacNamara's *The Valley of the Squinting Windows* (1919). For a start, only a few of these folk engage in the practice, and what gossip we do see is not malevolent but the result of understandable curiosity, as with the very generalized gossip concerning the competition for Brigid's hand — and, indirectly, for Neddie's farm (144, 148). Moreover, O'Donnell shows a certain sensitivity towards those characters of his that hide terrible secrets; there is no condescending laughter at gossiping Mrs. Brennans in O'Donnell's novel. Mary Nabla's privacy, for instance, is safe (91). I have already noted Mercier's comment about the relatively selfconscious nature of the writing in this book, and that that selfconsciousness is not always necessarily a flaw. O'Donnell clearly tries harder to "be" a writer in this novel by making many passages more "poetic" than is his usual wont. A positive effect is the occasionally deft onomatopoeia, as when peasant women are described as "sipping strong tea" and their nightly occupation as "the tinkle of dancing knitting needles" (3). Conversely, the juxtaposition of disparate ideas to "shock" the reader seems gratuitous and usually does not work well, as when we are told that "the morning was . . . dripping with the singing of birds" (31). O'Donnell's use of images to show the associations made in the consciousness of his characters, however, is always good. When Hughie returns to his townland after his stint in the Lagan, the image of a row of treasured eggs sitting on top of the dresser acts as a depressing force for him, reminding him of the degree of poverty around him; at some intuitive level, "the glug of the water under his feet in the spongy bog" suggests for him the row of eggs (87), but the fusing of these ideas is perfectly appropriate — for both symbolize the tenuous life led in his townland. Another recurring image worth mentioning is that of Mickey Sheila's horse "plunging" through the thin topsoil and foundering in the bog beneath (*e.g.* 292).

O'Donnell's stylistic selfconsciousness is definitely a positive trait in the novel. His narrator's reliance on subject-initiated simple sentences often produces almost a black-and-white cinematic effect: " A cloud of steam from the kettle was driving out into the middle of the floor. He lifted off the kettle and set it on the hearth close to the fire. He hung on a pot of potatoes to boil for the hens. Brigid came silently down from the room in her bare feet. She made no remark to her uncle. She washed her hands in the tin dish that rested on the bottom of an up-turned barrell at the gable. She did not wash her face. Her uncle was knuckling down the top row of potatoes so as to fit on the lid" (99).

And so ends the paragraph. The result here is particularly apt, given the sounds and stark mood in Brigid's kitchen — without any speech. Though some dialogue follows in the next paragraph, it is terse and purely functional — no different from the mood preceding it. In fact, the opening pages of this seventeenth chapter constitute a beautifully rendered portrait of an ordinary morning in a peasant cabin, with the details presented in relentless simple sentences. We gain a sense that O'Donnell is merely reporting what *is*, without embellishment and with only connotative interaction between sentences, a method occasionally used by Liam O'Flaherty, as in "Mackerel for Sale," for example. The characters' own sentences in dialogue are usually constructed in much more complicated fashion than the narrator's, a fact that leads me to conclude that the narrator's style has indeed been consciously honed; the clipped sentences minimize the connections that can be made for us by the distant narrator and encourage us to create our own perspective from the assemblage of facts provided—a technique that, of course, aids O'Donnell's "detached" sense of naturalism. The effort reminds one of Henry James's attempts to create a withdrawn narrator, only O'Donnell is, in a more limited way, more successful because he uses such short sentences. Such a style also invites the reader to greater participation, drawing him or her deeper into the scene that is being depicted. The O'Donnell chapter we have just now been discussing is also structured well, with a bookend conclusion when the day is done: there is no speech, not even a reflexive "goodnight" exchanged between uncle and niece (113). I must re-emphasize the starkness of this novel, a mood that is clearly enhanced and partially created by the attention paid to style. I should also add, finally, that sometimes the effect is so strong as to imply that — in truly naturalistic fashion — people, animals, objects, and the land itself are all somehow on an equal plane. Therefore, Hughie is "as much a part of the glen as the stream," and under Brigid's feet, thin ice can "tinkle. . . . like laughter" (162, 163). The suggestion is strong.

A word must now be said about O'Donnell's characterization, which is a virtue, especially in the first half of the book. I have already mentioned the likable Tommy Not'in' and Danny Rogers. To their number we may obviously add the hardworking Hughie himself as well as Neddie, but O'Donnell's creation of Brigid reaches deeper than that of any other character, although there are periods when we are told hardly anything at all about her. The parts of the novel that deal with Brigid's spiritual life are sensitively rendered, as when we feel her despair after surrendering her savings to Nellie: "What makes me feel helpless is that givin' Nellie me passage looks like if there'll be no escape from Adrigoole now. See the way them hills is all closed round us on three sides an' it's the sea makes the grey gap back there. That was the gap I was to go out thro'" (159). Brigid's claustrophobia in this glen society is partly caused by Mickey Sheila's constant insinuations regarding her, which threaten her deeply-rooted sense of independence.

Despite these various positive attributes, *Adrigoole* must be considered inferior to *Islanders* — though this may be, at least in part, because O'Donnell tries to do more in this novel and is therefore eligible to fail more often. Sometimes the novel appears flimsy because it moves too fast in crucial places — as in the rapid development of the love between Hughie and Brigid (207). Other times, especially towards the end, improbabilities of plot mar our enjoyment of the book, as when Hughie and Brigid both independently resolve to go to Scotland on the same night and meet on the same boat (172); when the poteen-makers' operation is discovered on the very first night Hughie joins them (294); and when Hughie arrives home from his seven months in jail *just* after Brigid has died (326-27). Such a headlong dash to bring the novel to a close is, unfortunately, not limited to *Adrigoole*; we shall see that the same is true of *The Knife*, which additionally lacks some of the virtues that serve to recommend *Adrigoole* — a novel that is ultimately satisfying enough, even if it is very uneven in quality. What we remember after having read the novel is the brilliance of the first half, which is strong enough to sustain our good opinion through the novel's inferior second half.

The Knife

In 1930 appeared O'Donnell's fourth novel, *The Knife*, which, though perhaps his best known, is far from being his best written. It is a historical novel dealing with Ireland's troubles during the Anglo-Irish war and Irish civil war — from a strictly local point of view in a Donegal townland. None of O'Donnell's novels has attracted more critical attention: Freyer has called it "the most dynamic . . . of all O'Donnell's novels"[27] and elsewhere hails it for conveying "with unusual verisimilitude the political experience of the Irish war"[28]; Fallis classifies it among the three O'Donnell novels that are "probably his best"[29]; Alan Warner feels it is one of the best novels he knows about the civil war[30]; and Brenda O'Hanrahan claims that it is a powerful account "of the growth of regional nationalism."[31] But many critics fall short of such praise, and rightfully so. Even Fallis must admit that "the novel is somewhat weakened by obvious melodrama and diffuse characterization,"[32] while Mercier goes further in arguing that it fails as "a unified work of art,"[33] not only for the reasons Fallis cites, but additionally for its desultory thematic pattern: when "one theme dies out . . . another has to be found to take its place."[34] More recently, Johann Norstedt has called it "an uneven novel, inferior to O'Donnell's other work" because it probably "attempts to do too much," for O'Donnell's various aims "do not blend together."[35] Its inferiority to the rest of O'Donnell's canon, with the possible exception of *Storm* and *Proud Island*, seems to me manifest: the novel simply has not withstood the test of time. Even then, *The Knife* is not entirely without some virtues.

Perhaps most impressive among these is its ability to demon-
strate the complex network of shifting allegiances that occurred
during the war years, for things were considerably muddier than
many history books would lead us to believe. Freyer has noted "the
deep crosscurrents of neighborliness and loyalties,"[36] where former rebel compatriots are pitted against one another,[37] a Free Sta-
ter helps a wounded Republican (210), a sympathetic government
jailer enables a rebel to escape (236), and the leader of a group of
Orangemen first hides fenians (111) and later rescues Republican
prisoners moments before they are to be shot (287).

The sense of flux is well rendered, from the opening, where we
see the servant class rising to take possession of land traditionally
held by Orangemen, to the time when the Orangemen can put
their weight behind Home Rule, which preserved their property
and some of their political clout (157). And when some tans murder an old couple for withholding information, the Orangemen —
as Irishmen — are outraged along with their rebel adversaries
(156). Norstedt has commended the novel for its "remarkably
even-tempered view of Orangemen,"[38] and he is quite right — for,
at the novel's close, even a love relationship between a fiery rebel
woman and a leading Orangeman is in the offing. Times were
changing rapidly, and O'Donnell shows us such changes, not only
on the more prominent social and political levels, but also on the
everyday level, as when we see two old men complaining about
such modern foibles as the lighting of pipes with matches instead
of with live coals, and the buying of socks in shops instead of their
being made at home (67).

Also well represented is the frustration of uncompromising, so-
cialist-minded rebels in the face of the Catholic establishment,
which was quite ready to compromise — often in pursuit of selfish
ends. The group that chiefly illustrates such behavior is the
Burnses, a rising Catholic family intent on profiting as much as
possible from the turbulence of the times. In many ways, the
Burnses suggest William Faulkner's Snopes family: after a slow but
gradual start they eventually come to infiltrate society at all levels.
Since "them that has least can burn most" (40), the Orangemen
fear reprisal as their once-absolute power by degrees begins to
erode and they are forced to compromise, even as their land is
overrun (155). Throughout, the Burns family is shown to be mor-

ally and ideologically pliable, first in the deal whereby James Burns
will be made local rate collector if a local Catholic family can be
persuaded to leave their newly-acquired land (42), and later when
James is rejected by Nuala Dhu, the fiery rebel woman, and joins
the Free State army as the local commanding officer (167). Once
the civil war begins, the friction between the Burnses and the rebels increases, beginning with the Dhu family disrupting Father
Burns's Mass when he uses the service as a political platform
(chapter 37), and later with the Dhus' house wrecked in a raid or-
dered by James Burns. In the latter case, it is emphasized that not
even the British used to do such damage in searching a house, and
the bitterness of civil war, with all its abuses, is tellingly brought
home as we see two old men on their knees gathering the stuffing
torn out of a mattress and preparing to stitch it all together again
(196). In keeping with the presentation of the complex allegiances
of the times, O'Donnell fittingly has Phil Burns, the family patri-
arch and the only Burns sickened by his family's repulsive behavior, as one of the old men on his knees in a rebel house. A final
point should be made regarding the Burnses and their local
power: much private information is passed on to the ruthless
James Burns by his sister, Mary, who in attending Father Burns's
house takes in all sorts of news useful to the Free State government
and serves as a kind of nerve center for the neighborhood gossip
network. Clearly, O'Donnell's sympathies lean more toward the
Orangemen, who are generally depicted as far more honorable
than the turncoat rebels now in power in the Free State.

These themes underlie a basic naturalism that seems to me inferior to what we have seen in previous O'Donnell novels. Although
Fallis finds the author's "control of naturalistic techniques . . . im-
pressive,"[39] he does not specify what those techniques are. Obviously, the presentation of the war-torn environment suggests
naturalistic forces at work, but, beyond that, little of the novel's
naturalism is well enough defined to be effective. Indeed, the only
other strong strain in the novel seems to be once again the chemical power of sexual attraction, as when James Burns feels himself
recklessly compelled to see Nuala Dhu, even though British soldiers and police are everywhere (117). Nuala herself is similarly
drawn, not to James or Dr. Henry, who also woos her, but to Sam
Rowan, leader of the Orangemen (278). In fact, the disruptive

power of Nuala's sexual attractiveness coerces all three suitors into betraying their ideals, to varying degrees: James rejects the rebel cause and becomes an enemy once he knows he cannot have her; Dr. Henry admits he took in Nuala's wounded brother, The Knife, merely in order to impress her, not out of any patriotic spirit or idealism; and even Sam Rowan's services to her cause — for instance, hiding fenians in his house — have been motivated by his desire for her, at the risk of outraging his own Protestant followers.

A technique that is obliquely suggestive of naturalism is O'Donnell's deft use of animal imagery to show apprehension and fear. Thus Billy White, the rash and psychologically unstable Orangeman, is likened to a setter, "halting with one foot raised" as he skulks through the woods (72); to a frightened cow in terms of the look in his eyes (72); to a squealing rabbit "under terror of a weasel" (73); and to "a wounded seal" in terms of the screams he lets out (109). Others are similarly compared, as when Andy Mor is said to be "like a curlew, frightened at everything that's going on" (151).

As we have seen, Fallis faults the novel for its "diffuse characterization," and indeed the characters *are* insubstantial — as flat as in Brinsley MacNamara's political novel, *The Clanking of Chains* (1919), and for the very same reasons: as representatives of certain *kinds* of people and forces, they are not well-rounded as individuals. Freyer excuses O'Donnell by arguing that "a character who correctly personifies a trend in history may teeter on the edge of becoming a marionette,"[40] but the key word here is the auxiliary verb: O'Donnell's characters *do* teeter, and in fact may arguably be classified as little more than puppets. Partially this is because so much of the novel is dialogue, and most of the remainder is narrative unhelpful in terms of character development — historical matter, for instance. It is even unclear why the novel is named after the character of The Knife, since substantial portions of the novel have nothing whatsoever to do with him. If he is the central figure, then that status can be accorded him only by the way of default; once again, nearly fifty years ago, Mercier was perfectly accurate in complaining that The Knife "fails to come to life at all."[41] And if the central character fails to do so, then what of the others? Dr. Henry and Sam Rowan are the next closest, as they are given several humanizing traits. Nuala follows, but after her we descend to a level where caricature is the most accurate term that can be applied.

But if the novel's characterization constitutes a bleak failure, then we can at least argue that several of the novel's scenes are brilliantly conceived and constructed. Norstedt has specifically termed "superb" the scenes of the rebels nervously hiding in a dugout and listening for signs from the outside world, and of the Dhus' confrontation with Father Burns during Mass.[42] Also worthy are the scenes revealing the point of view of hostages taken by the British for a few hours, and some of those that give us an impression of prison life. Still, the last section of the novel is poor in terms of its relationship to the rest of the novel. As Norstedt has observed, the end of the book is like "reading somebody's jail journal" rather than the conclusion of a well-constructed novel.[43]

The Knife does start out well in terms of plot and even character, but it very quickly deteriorates into a series of barely connected scenes that succeed only in showing realistic war situations — or anecdotes, as Mercier has termed them.[44] They have the flavor of what these war experiences must have been like, but as fiction the novel is, as a whole, without doubt, inferior stuff. A series of thematically unified short stories might have made better use out of such material — something like Corkery's *The Hounds of Banba*(1920), only O'Donnell's superior realism would likely have yielded a far better collection. Clearly, the germs of several good stories can be found within the pages of this episodic book, but as a complete novel *The Knife* stands, unfortunately, as perhaps the weakest piece in the O'Donnell canon.

On the Edge of the Stream

On the Edge of the Stream, published four years later, remains distinct from all else in O'Donnell's canon for two reasons. The first is the novel's often humorous bent, which Freyer sees as an adulteration, "an imposition of knockabout comedy from the out side";[45] however, such humor seems to me to be very similar to what Seumas O'Kelly earlier achieved in *Hillsiders* (1921), a short-story collection whose basic underlying themes are no less serious. Perhaps because of the novel's interesting dual nature, Mercier finds that it "is more enjoyable than any other of [O'Donnell's] novels except *Islanders*, and is better written and constructed than any."[46] The second distinguishing feature is the novel's overt socialist message, which never really does reach the level of outright propaganda the way Corkery's *The Hounds of Banba* frequently does. A socialist experiment and its effect on a rural community are the novel's primary subject matter, but that fact alone, of course, does not mean that *On the Edge of the Stream* is socialist propaganda. In many ways it is, rather, a criticism of certain sociological[47] patterns — as Mercier puts it, a struggle between "'progressive' movements" and "a combination of the Church and the bourgeoise."[48] The alliance of the Church with the well-to-do and the acquisitive is taken to task, as is the power these two groups can wield over the average, hardworking farmer.

The novel was written while O'Donnell lived on Achill Island in Mayo,[49] where Figgis had also gone a decade or so earlier. Adapting some factual events, O'Donnell transposed them to his usual Donegal setting and created a novel about a townland's attempt to run a cooperative store in the face of opposition from the local gombeen family and the clergy. As in O'Kelly's *Hillsiders*, the townland's houses are very near to one another — close enough that any small noise can "draw heads out of half a dozen doorways"[50] — which makes for close ties among neighbors; indeed, we come to know these people — each with his or her own individual quirks — quite well, a situation that helps cultivate the novel's humor. It should be noted that such humor tends to be very good-natured and kindly, as it is in *Hillsiders*, rather than mean-spirited as it so often is in MacNamara's best-known work. O'Donnell usually shows us the foibles of innocent or likable characters, so that the effect is more often than not gentle and heartwarming. Particularly funny episodes are Red Charlie and his drum (76); the lovable Donal Breslin dealing with his mule (152-54) and trying guiltily to finish his pint after the priest has entered the pub (91); and Nelly Joyce's frustration at trying to pump information out of Ouida Beag, an incredibly stupid country bumpkin (chapter 20). Sometimes the humor is farcical, as when Dan Boyle prepares to write a letter:

> He sat down to manoeuvre [sic] himself into his spectacles. One ear had to be bent down so that the first leg might slide into position. When that ear was free, he bent down the other and led the second leg to its place. But the first drew loose and the glasses swung across his face. With a slap of his palm he trapped them against his nose and firmly led the erring leg back, groaning as he stabbed recklessly for a grip of it around his ear. It held. The other leg held. He shook his head gently. They both held. And then with a grunt he grabbed a pen. It tripped, stuck one leg and scooted ink across the sheet. (18)

Dan's response to all this trouble is to give up and resolve instead to go out in search of a stiff drink. At this level end all parallels to O'Kelly's short-story collection, for where O'Kelly's concern is the nurturing and accepting sense of rural community, O'Donnell's is the desire of such communities to be led — the important question being who is to do the leading, disinterested farmers from among their number, or rapacious gombeen men and complacent priests who are self-interested?

The plot focuses upon Derrymore's co-op, or cope as it comes to be known, which is founded by Phil Timony and Dan Boyle and is housed in Phil's barn. Soon, Father Cassell is warning against the cope from his pulpit (chapter 23), to which Dan responds by arguing that priests were always too ready to give ear to the rich (145), meaning the Garvey family, whose power base of shopkeepers, attorneys, and priests awes the simple farmers (150). The cope's existence is, to the farmers, "dark, exciting, enjoyable . . . and sinful" (187), enlivening their spirits as they watch the Church mobilize against the cope and its backers. Ned Joyce organizes a procession — replete with priests, nuns, and banners — to surround Phil's house, but these forces are ignominiously routed when Donal lets his bull out of its field (207). Before long, the cope moves directly into the town of Carrick, where it is betrayed by its patrons, who fear doing business directly in front of the Garveys' shop (239). To capitalize on such intimidation, the shopkeepers and priest send for "The Holy Fathers," who will "give a mission' against the cope "(267); now more than ever, the lackeys surrounding the Catholic establishment puff themselves up by increasing the level of their servility before those who are in power, but all ends in chaos after Nelly's heartfelt speech to the throng, and the cope still stands when the novel concludes.

What matters most to us in this novel, however, is not the idea of the cope, nor the socialist lesson, nor even the portrayal of townland life; it is the character and fate of the suffering Nelly Mc-Fadden Joyce. She is the victim of an arranged marriage, whereby Ned Joyce was given his post as school principal if he agreed to marry her. More painful to her is the reality of having to lose her sweetheart, Phil Timony, who, heartbroken, leaves the townland. Nelly feels her spirit becoming steadily subdued by her inability to communicate with her egocentric husband and by her increasing lack of patience with her children — symptoms, really, of her isolation and boredom. To illustrate her spiritual emptiness, O'Donnell gives us some fine correlatives; for example, one night Nelly lies awake in bed after Ned has fallen asleep: "She became aware of the wind bugling in an empty bottle. It rang out at times in a weird howl, without feeling or life, or meaning of any kind, something lonely and lost beyond words"(48). Clearly, she too feels like an empty receptacle, drained by life of almost all meaningful content. After Phil returns twelve years later, she feels longings to see him, but is discouraged by her fear of gossip, for "in the

darkness of all the doorways there were eyes" (52), and for the first
time in O'Donnell's fiction we see a person fearing gossip as much
as anyone in MacNamara's *The Valley of the Squinting Windows*. The
idea, however, of seeing Phil again transforms her, making her
feel fresh, alive, and in some indeterminate way, hopeful, after
years of reticence, sullenness, and virtual somnambulism. On the
other hand, she feels no response toward her husband, whose
clumsy hugging makes her "stand quietly" (119), as if she were
merely accepting his affections as she would any other conjugal
duty — for Nelly is, to all outward appearance, a "good wife."

But her spiritual paralysis extends beyond her flimsy relationship with Ned, expressing itself in physical terms that draw out our
sympathy for her: "A great weariness weighed down her limbs.
Many a time she too had knelt at the foot of the cross, her mind
weighted with gloom she could not understand. She put a hand
against the wall and pushed herself erect. The sense of weighted
gloom clung to her during the evening. . . . Sunday drew near,
tightening in on her body so that she felt it in her breathing"(128,
129-30).

Often she feels a sort of "sulking of mind and body" (168), one
time outside church even wondering if her legs can carry her in,
and when she finds they will not, ends by "flopping down on the
family grave" in the adjacent cemetery (136). Nelly's recovery
from this disease of the heart gains momentum after she has a
brief, face-to-face meeting with Phil that puts "a swing in her body
that made her young again, and a brightening in her face as if the
sun was on it" (232). Of course, with a rekindling of her spiritual
fire, Nelly finds the effort of dealing with Ned on an everyday basis
more odious than ever, and the friction between them increases —
especially when Nelly finds herself siding with the farmers instead
of with her image-conscious husband, the leader among the shop-
keeper forces, whose power keeps him in office. And when Nelly
refuses to march in the procession — Ned's brainchild — it is not
long until he physically abuses her, apparently trying to choke the
spirit out of her, if we may judge by the bruises on her neck. Her
body responds with a new bout of paralysis: her "arms, fingers,
legs . . . were dead. The fingers had no feeling for the things they
touched. And then the legs moved away from her. At least she had
no thought what was happening" (234). Their next altercation

leads to a shower of unrestrained blows as the level of abuse esca-
lates; symptomatic of her physical lack of independence is a kind
of claustrophobia, a desire to be physically isolated and free from
unwanted touching. This understandable condition is best rendered in the novel's closing scenes, as when Nelly is leaving
church: "caught in the jam of bodies at the door she fidgeted. . . . it
annoyed her that her body should be jammed in among bodies.
Once outside in the air — it's like rushing into cold water, she reflected — she dashed towards a little mound to get space, and have
air all around her body" (281).

This moment is merely a brief respite for her, however, as the
scenes that follow put one in mind of the chaotic conclusion of Na-
thaniel West's *The Day of the Locust* (1939), with at least as much sociological symbolic power (282). Extremely disoriented, Nelly is
pushed along by the crowd, which, in the grips of religious fervor,
is milling along en route to the destruction of Phil's cope and perhaps the murder of Phil himself. This grim, in many ways impressionistic, scene is brought to a sudden halt when Nelly realizes
Phil's dangerous position and, with the help of some men upon
whose backs she is hysterically pounding, manages to get the
crowd's attention, persuading it of the terrible truth about the
amoral, hypocritical shopkeepers killing Donal's bull — that its
death was not a heavenly sign condemning the cope. Thus has she
freed herself, asserted herself, and the shopkeepers are defeated.
In keeping with the impressionistic quality of the ending, Ned is
lost in the crowd as he is lost to her life. It is unclear whether she
will leave him, but it appears likely; perhaps the point is irrelevant,
given the mortal blow she has struck against the cope's enemies,
which signals the total downfall of her husband. The deeper reality
of these chaotic scenes is firm enough: Nelly is free for the first
time in her life. The comic scenes that have framed the episodes
exposing her suffering throw her situation into greater relief and
act to emphasize its pathetic nature, which is not at all humorous
or farcical. About her situation throughout most of the novel Costello has observed that "life in the largest sense [goes] underground," with love becoming "a guerrilla,"[51] and that we must read
beyond her sexual choice to remain with Ned until the last few
pages and see her situation more as a subjugation of healthy life itself.

A few words should now be said about Nelly's husband, Ned
Joyce, and then about Phil Timony, the man with whom she is in
love. Ned is an insecure man consumed with a lust for power — a
combination that renders him not only a ludicrous figure, but a
dangerous and violent one as well. He is a stupid little tyrant in the
habit of "raising his heels off the ground" (*e.g.*, 178) — as if he wants
to be physically bigger than he actually is. Constantly raving about
showing Nelly (178) and the townland (176) "who's boss," he feels
a kind of impotence because he cannot tame his proud wife's developing sense of independence (she was a mere girl when he married her), even as he cannot crush the cope's independence from
the shopkeepers, who have appointed him their leader. That his
political problems are inextricably linked to his sexual life is made
perfectly clear in the scene in which he severely beats Nelly for the
first time; after she passes out, he kisses her and fondles her, saying "strange tender words" (257). Then he guiltily worries more
about what people will say if this secret is discovered than he does
about the condition of his wife, who is unconscious on the floor
before him (258). Considering this in some strange way a victory at
home, he becomes "like a drunken man" (269) at the prospect of
winning his war against the cope and thus rising — perhaps all the
way to a seat in Parliament, as he imagines (177). He even refers to
himself as "king" (270) prior to the grand disruption at the novel's
end, during which his wife's speech to the crowd finally defeats
him.

Not surprisingly, Phil Timony is the complete opposite of Ned
in terms of his robust physique and cool temperament. We first
see him upon his return to Derrymore, wearily trudging through
the streets during a severe rainstorm in order to see his dying
mother. He cuts a romantic figure, especially after it is learned
that he has walked fifty miles in such weather. In fact, the rain itself
and the recurring image of this "stranger" walking through it are
factors that serve to unify some early chapters (3-6), which take
place in a variety of locations; the use of this technique supports
Mercier's contentions about the novel's structural precision. Phil
is also truly heroic; unlike the cowardly, wife-beating Ned, who,
along with most of the procession's marchers, breaks ranks once
Donal's bull is released among them, Phil risks his life and saves
some petrified nuns from being gored by the bull's horns (208).

Nelly is further impressed by the heartfelt speeches Phil gives to
the farm folk —which contrast with Ned's calculated and prepared
talks (217). Clearly, Phil is all the things Ned cannot be: self-as-
sured, secure within himself, romantic, and fiercely independent
— as when he candidly observes he has "got out of the habit of
going to Mass" (67). A likable figure, Phil attracts our attention,
but he remains nevertheless very shadowy because we simply do
not see him enough; that is, he seems more an agent to liberate
Nelly from her husband and the townland from gombeenism than
he is a fully developed character in his own right.

Better developed are the lovable Donal Breslin and his doings,
which draw our affection toward this good-natured, unselfish
man. Father Cassell is also a dim figure for most of the novel until
near the end, when O'Donnell pays him careful attention and we
see Cassell emerge as a shrewd multi-dimensional character who is
not the easily-manipulated fool Ned Joyce has led us to believe he
is. O'Donnell is, in fact, better at rendering character in this novel
than in any of those preceding it; he is more introspective — or
rather allows his characters to be, as in this scene, after Nelly has
joyfully become aware of Phil's return: "There was no new sound
in the night around her. What was strange was the change in herself. She was no longer weighted down and old. She got up carefully, wondering whether she could trust this mood to the hazard
of a movement. She did, and it held. She even shook her head, and
it held"(55).

The misery of unhappily married women is carefully explored
in the novel, not only through Nelly, but also through other examples, such as Mrs. Miller, the wife of the local doctor, who is an al-
coholic: "When they went in Smullen's [pub], the eager life
emptied out of her flesh and left her limp and tired, a fair-haired
woman hiding her grey hairs just as she disguised her frayed
clothes; a soft-faced woman with a patient smile. . . . he and she
were strangers without eyes or ears to peer into the life around
them. . . . At times the cold unfriendliness of the world cowed
her"(89). Clearly, Mrs. Miller feels the same sense of alienation as
the fully-developed Nelly.

In large part, O'Donnell's characters reveal themselves to us so
well because of the narrator — as much because of his well-timed
absences as because of his presence. That is, technically, I suppose,

we are sometimes given narrated interior monologue but often in this novel the narrator is only barely there, adding an occasional comment; not infrequently, he is hard to detect at all and the musings of a character come through as if directly. Thus do we see into the mind of Smullen the publican, who is here reflecting on Dr. Miller's son, a clerical student: "John James Michael could go to hell. Like enough the Garveys had him on a string. Well, be damned to him, standing there sniffing like a dog at the mouth of a burrow; fungus-faced bastard, with no more life in him than a pasty plant starved for sunlight. If that cub starts talking. . ." (92; ellipsis is O'Donnell's).

To be fair, this quote is only part of a long paragraph in which a narrator occasionally reveals himself. At other times, however, we find entire paragraphs with no detectable narrator at all. In this case, it is Nelly worrying about her recently returned former sweetheart: "Phil Timony should run away. He should clear. He should run. Somebody should tell him to run. But who would tell him? Nobody would look at him once his name was read out off the altar, a man like him that didn't go to Mass. What does he care? And what do I care? It's nothing to me what happens to anybody. Can't I mind my own business . . .?" (129).

But most often we do find such monologues embedded in larger narrative structures, as in the following paragraph, which is representative of what is the more typical method of presentation. Here we are given quotation, narrative observation, narrative commentary, and interior monologue: "'Queer that that dog should die, and that the bull should be stricken, too.' Nelly spoke no word. He noticed that she spoke no word. He rubbed his hands vigorously together. Did be hear the jingle of drops? He glanced out the window. The glass was clear. Funny the way thoughts get mixed. This was great. Nelly was the best cut of a woman in the countryside" (255).

Such passages serve to humanize Ned somewhat, make him less the buffoon — which, in turn, makes his violence towards his wife even more contemptible and therefore more provocative and engaging than if we were merely told of what would otherwise likely be a virtual caricature's actions, presented entirely from the outside. Ellipses are frequently used to give some indication that interior monologue is occurring or ending, but not in all cases, as we can see in the passage quoted above.

At times the interesting narrator muses as if he were a character in the novel (*e.g.*, 168), poses questions to his reader, and even renders the collective consciousness of a group of farmers: "And listen: would Michael Boyle go so far as to drive back the bullocks? The Boyles are hasty. No heed should be put in thon talk. Not but Father Cassell was a botheration. Many a time a man's grass was little enough for himself; though them that refused had no luck with their own cattle. Damnation, if it wouldn't madden ye to have Phil Timony raising all this in yer mind, and leaving you there to box at it; on a Sunday, too, when yer mind had no backing"(144).

And with equal dexterity, the consciousness of the women folk is rendered: "Be damn to him, what right had he to get up there before the play-actors and the penny-boys of The Town and make out that country people were in such want? Wouldn't talk like that make your blood boil? It was the men started it all — wouldn't men vex you? And now they were gone out into the fields, rooting and digging, heavy headed with their drink" (105).

The entire twenty-fifth chapter is dedicated to exposing the thinking of the townland's women, who, albeit often behind the scenes, wield a considerable amount of power in Derrymore. Sometimes their inward consciousness is rendered when the narrator draws our attention to outward signs. For instance, quite frequently the emotions women feel are communicated through the use of what I call "the rhetoric of knitting needles": the clicking sounds the needles make can be interpreted as anger (58), uncertainty (61), courageousness (61), scowling (63), friendliness (65), and, when they stop altogether, shock (67). In the last case, when they resume their commentary, the narrator asks, "did you ever hear knitting needles cheer" (67); we also know they can "duel" back and forth with so much vehemence that it is sometimes "hard to say which needles won" (158). Clearly some humor is intended here, but the issues upon which the women comment are often quite serious.

O'Donnell also uses animal imagery effectively to help render his characters, a technique that he first employed on a broad scale in *The Knife* and that is extended and more richly textured in *On the Edge of the Stream*. Fowl imagery is most common. Thus Ouida the simpleton is described as having "blue eyes, faded like a robin's eggs" (103), her voice as "chirruping" (124), and her intellect as having "a dim-minded power to peck at what went on around her; [sic] like a sparrow nebbing at specks among gravel" (129). Visiting neighbors "scatter into the fields like hens that go leisurely out after a shower" (51), and even Phil's waterlogged boots produce a sound like "the guttering of a feeding duck in the shallow edge of a pond" (35). Domestic pets also figure prominently in the imagery, as when the doctor's son is described as "standing there sniffing like a dog at the mouth of a burrow" (92), and people suspect that Phil will be put "out of the country . . . the way you'd put a dead kitten on a shovel" (107). Large farm animals, not surprisingly, play a significant part: Donal's eyes are "large and brown and kindly like a cow's" in registering wonder (154); married couples endure "the dull teamstering of draft animals," an image that is deftly extended throughout a long paragraph (167); and the endearingly independent Briany McFadden is compared to a donkey because "a donkey will just stick his rump into a hurricane, put down his head and weather squalls that . . . . strip houses" (276). Not all references can be classified, but it is clear that all are homely, non-exotic images that are subtly woven into the novel's fabric. For instance, no one is ever "hungry as a bear" or "angry as a lion."

On the Edge of the Stream is a carefully written novel that should please most readers. Its variety in terms of subject matter, method of presentation, and tone is its strength, and it has no glaring shortcomings. The impressionistic final scenes are masterfully created and memorable, almost cinematic in that they record so much activity — different from the almost still-life, photographic qualities that characterize *Islanders* or *Adrigoole*. The tone, in shifting back and forth between the farcical and the pathetic, keeps us as engaged as if we were reading a Shakespearian play, where Nelly's spiritual and physical suffering constitute a powerful main plot and the issue of the cope is merely a comic subplot—relief from the scenes where Ned vents his unthinking cruelty upon his wife. We care about these characters in a way that was impossible in *The Knife*, because here they have been painstakingly drawn and are at least as important, if not more so, than thematic exposition. *On the Edge of the Stream* is a very good novel, perhaps on the same level as *Islanders* in terms of literary quality, even if it is a more self-conscious work relative to the raw power of the earlier novel. It is to be hoped that before long we will see a new edition, for the novel simply does not deserve to be forgotten, especially when inferior, though historically important, work such as *The Knife* is seeing new editions.

The Big Windows

The Big Windows, published twenty years after the last of his early novels, is probably O'Donnell's greatest single literary achievement; it also happens to be the novel O'Donnell himself has called his "best."[52] Freyer has rightly called it "the most complex" of O'Donnell's novels,[53] even though it maintains a surface simplicity that is inextricably a part of O'Donnell's vision of rural Ireland. Few critics, however, include any discussion of *The Big Windows*. Fallis, for example, not only omits the novel entirely from his review of O'Donnell's work, but fails to include it (and *On the Edge of the Stream*, by the way) in his list of O'Donnell's best three novels while, surprisingly, he does make room for the flawed novels *Adrigoole* and *The Knife*.[54] But apparently enough general interest exists, I am glad to say, to warrant a brand-new edition [55] of this compelling novel, which sensitively chronicles the passing of "the Ireland of the cloistered glen"[56] around the turn of the century.

Although it is set during the years of the Boer war, the novel's location is familiar from *On the Edge of the Stream*; the townland's name has changed from Derrymore to Glenmore , but Carrick remains as the central hub of townland affairs. Even this far back in time, the Garveys are the established shopkeepers, ever "the rogues and robbers of Carrick."[57] The farmers from the surrounding countryside, as before, see the shopkeepers as a snobby crowd, always putting on airs and being overly concerned with vague proprieties (208). Because of its extreme isolation — unusual even for Donegal — the townland is a strange place with stranger customs that have been developing virtually undisturbed for centuries. In part because of these reasons, there is room for humor here too, but it is far less farcical than in *On the Edge of the Stream*, more involved with the idiosyncratic quirks of the community's members. For instance, we have the case of Briany and his dog, to whom Briany has given so many different names that the dog responds to the call of any name — which, of course, means that any neighbor calling his own dog will find himself dealing with Briany's as well. Tom Manus is said to be able to "piss punch" (101) after drinking a load of whiskey, and Bella is described as "a useless big lump . . . with an arse on her like the end of a rick of hay" (146). The relative irreverence works well, sparking the novel to a more inclusive level of realism. One more general comment should be made here regarding O'Donnell's presentation of Glenmore: it is very much an adult-centered vision with a noticeable lack of individually identifiable children; virtually without exception, references seem always to be to anonymous groups of children whose play takes them up and down the glen.

Into this strange — even anachronistic — townland arrives young Brigid Dugan, newly married to Tom Manus. Brigid, an island woman, has no notion of the townland's unusual ways, and in a truly macabre scene is greeted that first dark night by eerie screeching and sharp words amid a bombardment of earth clods (18-19). Quickly hurried inside Tom's house, she is warmly received by Mary, her mother-in-law, who must explain that these are the actions of the townland women, women who resent the arrival of any strangers. And thus does O'Donnell broach his main theme: Brigid must slowly learn what is "the right thing to do" (98) on all levels; on the other hand, it is not long before Brigid is teaching the townland some sensible and compassionate new ideas of her own —for this educational experience will cut both ways.

Brigid is the novel's focal character, a woman with her fair share of normal human frailties but whose courage, open-mindedness, and capacity for love distinguish her from the novel's many reflexively conservative characters, who are generally submissive before townland customs — some of which are cruel, barbaric, and senseless. For instance, it is up to Brigid to challenge superstition and call for a doctor to tend a seriously ill child that would die without professional help; to save the girl's life, Brigid must first convince her neighbors that the child is not receiving a "punishment" for her mischief (213). In fact, no doctor has ever visited Glenmore until Brigid persuades the townland women of the boon a doctor can be in delivering children (142), and, as things turn out, Brigid's own complicated delivery requires the attention of a doctor, without whom, it is intimated, both mother and child might have lost their lives (179-81). Finding little patience for townland ways, Brigid is refreshingly direct, prone to confront local disagreements and prejudices with the desire to make peace, to clear things up — instead of permitting pernicious dislikes and hatreds to gnaw away at people, sometimes for years or even decades, without any real communication, all due to personal pride or social convention. After settling various strongly-felt domestic disturbances, she eventually develops a reputation as the glen's peacemaker (163).

Perhaps most telling of all, however, is Brigid's intercession on behalf of Ann the Hill, a simple, psychologically distracted woman who roams furtively around the glen, hiding behind creels and bushes, screeching in a high-pitched voice, and frightening both children and adults with her shocking behavior. With the tacit approval of the glen's adults, children form gangs that cruelly harass Ann, pursuing her and throwing clods of earth at her. But Brigid treats Ann as she would any other friend, always accepting her and defending her in the face of townland misunderstanding and narrowmindedness — for the prevailing opinion is that Ann should be disposed of by being sent to an asylum. Brigid's reactions, which are spontaneous and heartfelt, are an indicator of her breadth of vision — tolerant, loving, nurturing. When Ann is one day pursued and harried until she loses consciousness and eventually dies, it is a terrible loss to Brigid, who sorrowfully stays alone with the body all night, laying it out and preparing it for the funeral. It is during this process that Brigid discovers "a lump the size of . . . two fists" (193) under Ann's breast — the cause of her pain-induced shrieking and psychological imbalance. Where the community has failed to support one of its own, Brigid has accepted that individual and helped to make Ann's final years a little more bearable. Later on, after Tom is killed in a meaningless accident, Brigid decides to leave the glen, with her son, and return to island life — a choice that is practically mourned by the glen dwellers, who have come to feel great love for her.

Throughout the novel, the difference in perspective between island life and glen life is meaningfully explored. Most obviously that difference manifests itself in geographical terms, which are often symbolic: Brigid at first finds that the surrounding mountains have a suffocating effect on her, shutting out "the best part of the sky," and limiting her ability to judge the weather (22). As Brigid herself puts it: "An island is not like a glen. There is more sky over an island. The sea itself is like a turnover of the sky. There is more light on an island; inside a house and outside a house there is more light" (31).The lack of light indoors eventually becomes for her an enormously inhibiting factor, with symbolic overtones regarding the glen's closed-mindedness and backwardness.

But eventually, Brigid becomes acclimated to life in the glen, and her quietly devoted husband, Tom, realizes the final difference that the installation of big windows would make in improving the quality of her life. He has seen the big windows that are common in island cottages, windows that permit a flood of light to enter and enliven a home. After considerable discouragement and some stiff argument from Mary, his mother, the windows are installed, replacing the traditionally tiny windows of glen cabins. One can see why O'Donnell gave his novel its name, for the windows serve as a nexus for the novel's most important themes and as a correlative for the novel's substance. Most significantly, the installation of the windows symbolizes the end of Brigid's ostracism from the community, whose members gladly aid Tom in the work required to put them in. Also important is Mary's capitulation to the will of her son and daughter-in-law, the latter of whom is now her equal instead of seeming at times her subordinate. And, of course, the windows symbolize Tom's great love for Brigid — a woman whose goodness he has always recognized and for whom he would do anything, regardless of the weight of the glen's disapproval. On another level, the windows also are symbolic of the light of progress that Brigid has brought to the once-intractable glen; she has shown that change is not always to be feared and that the expression of individuality can be a spiritually healthy part of life. And finally, the windows stand for the very joy of life that Brigid has brought with her into the moody, austere glen; lives that were once dark and torpid have become bright, as if filled with a sort of inner light. This is why Brigid's departure at the end of the novel is mourned by the glen dwellers almost as a death would be, as if a light had been put out of their lives. It should be noted that not all aspects of glen life are negative relative to island life: for instance, Brigid comes to love the songbirds of the glen, and "laments" that "all the birds that throng the strands of [her] island should have so little music in them" (114).

Along the way, O'Donnell shows us many endearing quirks of glen life, quirks that often serve to draw Brigid closer to her initially hostile environment. What value, for example, can be attached to an old nail? When Brigid's windows are about to be installed, Mary begs all "to bear in mind the nail below the lamp" because it is where her husband once used to hang his mirror when he shaved; emotional memories are thus summoned and are expressed in implicitly personified terms — "she would be lonely now without that nail" (88) — that suggest a mild fixation. Also curious to Brigid is the glen's tendency to have only one of any important item, which must then be shared by the entire glen. There is only one gun, for instance (124), and when Brigid brings a fishing net with her to the glen, it is cause for scandal at the mere thought that it is unique: does Brigid intend to share this treasure (39)? One more case is worth adducing: the townland's tendency eventually to work its way naturally toward peace after any "sudden departure from pattern," after which it "measures itself against [the] new reality." The glen's "old, old dislike for strangers" (93) — even if frightening and alienating — is, then, merely a temporary impediment that can be overcome with some effort on each side, as Brigid herself eventually proves true.

Some of the strangeness Brigid encounters has to do more properly with the glen's unusual mores. The many cases presented by O'Donnell bring the townland to life and help us feel at times almost as alienated as Brigid herself. Sometimes it is chapters after someone has taken offense that we discover the exact nature of Brigid's unintentional transgression. Brigid's very appearance in Glenmore, as Tom's wife, is one such trespass that we do not realize until later in the book—only when Brigid realizes it. That the glen has a deep dislike for strangers is only a partial explanation for why she is ostracized and threatened. In fact, Brigid endures a good measure of strangely antagonistic behavior before she is enlightened as to its cause: the first few women she meets by chance "raise their elbows and, prodding the air with them, walk away" from her at a brisk pace (21); Susan Dan gives Brigid "the evil eye" by laying "her hand flat against her face" and drawing "the skin down from under her eyes, flashing the red of them at Brigid" (25); and at Mass, the townland women twice "stampede" (43) against Brigid *en masse*. Brigid's only "fault" in incurring such behavior is that she has "plucked out of [the glen] the likeliest man it ever raised, a man the women of [the] glen had their eye on from [sic] he got into long trousers" (48). With few eligible men in Glenmore, the townland's women particularly resent losing the best of them to an outsider. Later on, when Brigid is more accepted by the community, the installation of the big windows produces puzzling behavior in Mary, who has up to this point been Brigid's staunchest defender; before Mary has capitulated, the mere talk of such windows sends her "to bed, her face to the wall, her outer skirt turned up over her head," with her rosary beads in her hand (72). This is Mary's attitude until her discussion with Tom settles the stalemate between Mary and her daughter-in-law.

Clearly, this is a very codified society. When Brigid finally makes her peace with Susan Dan, her most vigorous opponent, an exact procedure must be rigorously pursued: Susan must visit Brigid to borrow something she does not really need, in this case a cup of sugar; Mary then instructs Brigid on the parallel return: "Now it will be your turn to go in to Susan's and say to Susan you ran out of cream-o'-tartar. Susan will know you have no shortage of cream-o'-tartar, but this is the only time there will be any need of let-on between you. The be-all of neighborliness is to ask and to give. Susan knows that. You will show her you know that, too, when you go to her" (105).

One other lesson learned by Brigid worth mentioning here is Mary's admonition that one must not be too generous, as the sapper's wife once foolishly was:

She brought a riches of things into this glen. She showed people this, and she showed them that, and if you praised a thing she would force it on you, but she never asked anybody for anything. So they all took and they took and the more she gave the lighter they spoke of her, and it was not long till they were laughing at her. They ended up stealing everything they could lay hands on belonging to her, one afraid the other would get ahead of her, and in the end she had not a friend among them. You have to keep an eye on your neighbour — good watching will make good neighbours anywhere — and you have to keep your eye on yourself. (106)

A sense of propriety and balance seems to be essential to glen life — even down to the level of physical adornment, for Peggy Donal is afraid of Brigid's earrings (46).

The novel's rich texture includes a generous selection of interesting Glenmore traditions, most of which jar with the island traditions to which Brigid is accustomed. Brigid's neighbors in the glen, for instance, claim to know a tradition that keeps their cattle healthy, while the islanders, ignorant of such knowledge, do not fare nearly as well: when a cow kicks up a piece of flint, it is called a "fairy dart," and such articles should be carried home "to make them up in a small sack to be kept under a rafter in the byre" (56). In other cases, men are actually expected to get drunk on the first day of lime season (134-35); a woman must never go back to her own people to have her first child (143); and when a new house is erected, an elaborate tradition must be followed, so complex that it cannot be concisely summarized (204-06). Perhaps most intriguing is the tradition of the women's court: "At her first turf-cutting, after her marriage, a woman has to give a meal to all the women that care to gather round her, and that they make it a special kind of an affair. They do their best to anger her. . . . It is a kind of a court the women hold, and one woman is picked to ask questions and two to stand over you with heather besoms and to beat you on the legs, if you boggle at a question, and if you run they will follow you" (145). Men are permitted to know almost nothing about this tradition, and a lad who once dared hide in the attempt to learn more was caught, stripped naked, and beaten (146). Brigid survives the ordeal quite well when it comes her turn.

A wealth of folklore suffuses the novel as well. Some of it is presented in the form of ancient stories, as in the long account of how the "women's court" tradition began (146), and in the story of the man who used to bark like his dog — despite warnings not to do so — and who died when his dog died (114-15). The glen has its own version of "The Prophecy of Colmcille," which Sean Mor has learned by heart in the oral tradition (58-9), and which the glen dwellers indignantly defend as a fact, not a story — another *faux pas* committed by the newly-arrived Brigid. Interesting also is the precise amount the men can drink at a baptism — only what they can swallow in "five bobs of the Adam's apple" (99). Colorful folk remedies abound: to relieve the pain of Sean Mor's bleeding eyes, Brigid is instructed to pour cold tea into a spoon and let drops run off her little finger into his eyes (64-5); thorns are the best cure for warts (142); and if a woman's labor pains are extreme enough, "the greatest charm in the world" is "the death struggle of two live cocks buried in a hole in the ground" (167). The importance of such lore to these glen people is underscored when Brigid, who at this point is still largely scorned, fills in a missing blank in a folk tale that, though actually widely known, is believed by her neighbors to be unique to the glen: Brigid is highly praised and profusely thanked for sharing the words of a long-lost prayer, the missing part of the folk tale. It is only fitting that, following her departure from the glen about which she has learned so much and to which she has contributed so much, Brigid herself is "on her way to becoming folklore by the time [her] story is set down" (222).

As in his two preceding novels, O'Donnell employs a good deal of animal imagery, most of it once again pertaining to fowl and other domestic animals, although a new strain, dealing with sea creatures, is also prominent —in order to include Brigid's island experience. The general quality of the images is about equal to what it was in *On the Edge of the Stream*, only fewer of the images seem especially appropriate to the context in which they appear. Still, some are as good as any we have studied previously in O'Donnell's work. Briany's metaphor for the newly-arrived Brigid's anomie, especially as it results from her treatment at the hands of the glen's women, is worth quoting: "If you buy a cow and take her into this glen, it is strange, but you have to stand by her with a rod in your hand till the other cows come up to her, and sniff her, and lick her, and maybe push at her a bit with their heads, and you may have to do that for long enough before they take up with her" (28). This homely comparison is effective in illustrating — both for Brigid and for us — the puzzling social situation that is proving so painful. But perhaps the most striking image of all is that of Black Donal's brother, Hughie, who, while drunk, falls off a wagon one night and is found "dead in the morning, the big hailstones like bird's [sic] eggs in his [open] mouth" (159).

When we turn to stylistic matters, we see that although the dialogue continues to be as realistic and convincing as ever, the prose used by the narrator is remarkably different from anything we have seen in O'Donnell's previous novels:

> And then suddenly there it was, the warning smoke over the grey flags. 'Cheer let you, and shout.' They closed in on Miley Dugan's, with their melodeons and tin whistles, their fiddles and their antics, and their mildly bawdy talk, and they surged round Brigid and warned her to show signs of her feeding soon, and to make place for other island girls near her, and Brigid held her own with them and the procession and the confusion crossed the green to the creek, and Brigid stepped lightly into the boat. She put her back to the mast and her shawl slipped from her shoulders and she laughed back into the great uproar of their send-off. (11-12)

Such a flowing style is a prevalent trait in the novel, the repeated use of the coordinating conjunction "and" suggesting an attempt on O'Donnell's part to imitate the "melodic line" of the later stages of George Moore's literary career, during which Moore wrote and rewrote novels so as to create a similarly flowing effect. I cannot fathom Freyer's thinking, therefore, when he argues that in *The Big Windows* "O'Donnell's style . . . has now a slow reflective rhythm"[58] — for there is nothing slow and reflective in these sentences that sometimes tear along at relatively breakneck speed. If we compare these long, flowing sentences to the clipped, almost muted sentences of *Adrigoole*, we can see in these extremes the range of O'Donnell's stylistic experimentation. Once he had the luxury of writing at a leisurely pace in non-hostile surroundings, he was able to offer the same care to the development of his style as he did to the thematic force of his novels, creating styles more in harmony with content. The starkness of life presented in *Adrigoole* demanded a terse style; the emphasis on social interconnections in *The Big Windows* requires a greater flow that is capable of creating an instant network of frequently emotional associations, especially once the setting shifts from the island to the glen. A brief word should be said about another stylistic point, involving O'Donnell's use of ellipses: it is different from MacNamara's method in that O'Donnell's ellipses occur almost always at the end of a paragraph, signaling either a change of scene or a continuation of a conversation about which we do not need to know or whose conclusion we can foresee for ourselves. Never are they used in an attempt to help render a character's flow of thoughts.

The greatness of *The Big Windows* lies primarily in its ability to involve the reader in Brigid's social anomie and in having us learn the intricate complexities of glen life even as Brigid must. We share her anger, confusion, and sorrow as she becomes acclimated to such a life; we sympathize with her in a world where common sense matters little and where, instead, often-frustrating traditions are sometimes mindlessly followed and stubborn pride clouds almost everything. Progress in any form — whether in the shape of a doctor or an approaching railroad line — is resented and resisted. The contrasting character of the sensible, confident, and loving Brigid is admirable, as is her relationship with her mother-ln-law, through whom most of the learning and adjusting takes place. In fact, Mary's role in Brigid's education must not be underestimated: without Mary for support, Brigid would in all likelihood fail in her necessary attempt at assimilation into glen life. The glen's backwardness, once typical of western Ireland, makes it nearly unique; in Freyer's words, *"The Big Windows* is O'Donnell's epitaph on a way of life"* — one whose "social context he understood better than any writer of his generation."[59] It is to O'Donnell's credit that much of what must have been nostalgic for him to recreate is realistically shown with all its foibles and faults — and without any undue sentimentality. *The Big Windows* is a disciplined work that provides a wealth of detail about glen life, in effect recreating that life for the modern reader to marvel at and to enjoy. For these reasons and the sheer power of the story told, it is a work that will endure.

Proud Island

A sharp drop in quality is apparent when we come to O'Donnell's next novel, *Proud Island* (1975), although this book, too, is not entirely without merit. It is certainly *not* "probably [O'Donnell's] most tremendous achievement to date," as the *Sunday Press*'s Michael D. Higgins proclaims on the glossy cover of the O'Brien Press edition. If anything, it is a skeletal version of the best of O'Donnell's preceding novels, for many of the same themes and concerns are in evidence.

The major theme of pure idealism pitted against a dirty practicality is by now a familiar one in the O'Donnell canon. Hughie Duffy, the central male character, is an idealist, as are his wife and the devoted Dublin students who try to save the island from the pollution of crass real-estate incursions. In fact, Hughie compares the students to those who, like him, opposed the Dublin government because of its abandonment of idealism in favor of sullying compromises.[60] The students land on the island in an effort to prevent land sales and the sprouting of "no trespass" signs in the West, where such strict rules of ownership have never been seen. In spite of the invasion of Hughie's island by strangers, the islanders persist in their old, community-oriented ways — as when, during a storm, the strangers' boat is saved by the local fishermen (73).

I suppose Hughie is a heroic figure, albeit a thin one. One incident in particular thus defines him: after a storm has passed, Hughie goes back out on the ocean in the hope that the rough weather may have driven the herring shoals closer to the island, but while he is out the storm regathers and his boat is lost — last seen heading out to sea in an effort to warn a less-astute neighbor's crew that the weather is again threatening (88). Hughie's death provides the impetus his wife, Susan, needs to leave the island for good; her indomitability is demonstrated in her decision not to sell her land to crass real-estate developers — but rather to leave it unused after she arranges to have her cottage torn down (116).

The idea of emigration is strong throughout the book. Many of the islanders can no longer be appeased by the island's natural beauty and sense of ancient community (113-14), seeing instead only the harsh realities of financial insecurity and limited opportunities — for fishing is about the island's only real source of earned income, and with the loss of the herring shoals, such insecurity is more strongly felt than ever. This is why many resent the students' arrival, which they see as posing a threat to their chances of selling their land as the means of securing their passage abroad. But beyond drawing our attention to the problem, the novel does little to show any relief in sight — especially after Susan emigrates, taking her four children with her. Clearly, O'Donnell is pessimistic about the future of western Ireland, no matter how proud these islanders may be.

As usual, O'Donnell is effective in showing local traditions at work. In one case, we learn the method for claiming any wreckage that washes up on shore: all a man has to do is "gather a few handfuls of sand and lay them on it to have his claim put beyond question," but if an incoming wave washes away his sand, he loses all rights (76). One other tradition, of keening the dead who have drowned, is worth mentioning because the proud Susan Duffy will not comply with it — another sign of her spirited independence (91). Folklore is again featured as a prominent part of island life, as seen on "All Souls night" — one of "the two nights of the year when families keep to their owns firesides," talking of the dead, building new fires instead of raking the old, and saying the rosary (74).

The novel employs a first-person narrator by implication (use of "our," for example, 8), although for the most part this is a barely detectable trait. As in *On the Edge of the Stream*, however, the narrator occasionally lapses into bursts of interior monologue: "Is it trouble to us you would make her out to be? Well indeed she is no such thing. All we do for her when all is said and done is to see that there is a full creel of turf at the weather door at nightfall, a bucket of spring well water on the block of wood by the dresser and that the doors to her hen and duck houses are shut; children's work, all of it" (32). The immediately succeeding sentence returns us to conventional third-person narration. It is perhaps unfortunate that O'Donnell did not develop this technique to a greater extent, for, although infrequent, such passages enliven the book, giving it a greater sense of immediacy in the passages where it occurs. The author's choice — about when and where to use it — appears to be random.

A plethora of unfortunate errors mars the text, though these are probably the fault of publisher rather than author. For instance, if we do not count the period at the end of a sentence, O'Donnell's ellipses can have four marks (35), five (26), or even six (125). Misspellings are frequent: "her's" (71) and "one women glanced at the other" are but two examples.

In concluding, I can say only that *Proud Island* is too shallow and diffuse to be recommended, for it hardly seems to come alive for us at all. The novel's best part comes after Hughie's death, but much of its power replicates what Synge so perfectly achieves in *Riders to the Sea* (1904), to which O'Donnell's narrator refers directly (96). In many ways the novel is simply too familiar within the context of O'Donnell's entire canon — a story of close-knit neighbors living in a Donegal townland. The author seems creatively exhausted, fleshing out relatively little of his bony outline. For instance, aside from one chapter spent in Hughie and Susan's house one evening, we are given very little to make their relationship seem genuinely vital. The notion of islander pride is strong throughout, but is convincingly demonstrated only toward the very end, when Susan refuses to sell her land. *Proud Island*'s matter seems better suited to the short-story form; as a novel, it is just stretched out too thin.

The Short Stories

Judging by the quality of O'Donnell's three short stories, all published in *The Bell*, we can only regret that he did not pursue this form more often, for his stories are very attractive indeed — concise, well structured, and engaging in the same simple way as his best novels. Each employs a powerful image around which the rest of the story revolves; two of these startling images are strong enough not only to sustain the stories, but also to remain with us long after we have experienced them.

"Remembering Kitty"[61] is the lightest of the three stories. A first-person narrator, recollecting the days of his own boyhood, paints a vignette of his townland's chief gossip, Kitty. O'Donnell's portrait reveals once again an attitude toward gossips that is far kinder than MacNamara's, for here we have an affectionate, tolerant remembrance — warts and all. Although feared, Kitty is accepted as part of the community. Her three apparently irresponsible sons "drift" — the recurring descriptive term — around but contribute nothing toward her survival; she lives in a kitchen that has never had a room added to it, though structural preparations have at some distant time been made to allow for just such a possibility. The narrator is sympathetic to Kitty's position as well as accepting of her nature: that is, it is not Kitty's fault if she is a gossip. Her demeanor merely betrays the emptiness in her life, a void that, at least in the material sphere, is temporarily relieved by way of an inheritance, but when the money runs out, she returns to being a "terror" once again to her community.

The story's principal image is well-conceived: "Kitty touched the road like a gramophone needle entering on a record." Contained within it is Kitty's relentlessness, her fixed route, and the fact that she "explodes" with sound at every door she darkens; also reflected are her almost mechanical rate of travel and her lack of sensitivity toward her neighbors, which is also on the level of a machine.

"Why Blame the Sea Gulls?"[62] also employs a first-person narrator, probably to create a sense of immediacy once again. Structurally, the story falls into three distinct parts. The first is about the spotting of a sinking ship off the west coast of Ireland and about the rescue boats going out and the men boarding the mysterious vessel. The second part is about the discoveries made on board: it is an abandoned cargo ship — "The war had sent us a prize" — loaded with timber, a rare commodity; the ship is unloaded of as much as possible before it finally sinks. The last part is concerned with the discovery of a floating human body before the boarders can reach shore, a body "whose face is tilted backwards" and whose eyes have been pecked out by seagulls; where once these birds were "part of the joy of the day," they now become hated objects at which stones are thrown by those who have seen or heard of the body.

The central idea is of modern war reaching everywhere and blighting life on many levels. Now "no man stands on the cliff-top and looks out, without dread, over the wide wastes of the bay." There is a certain loss of innocence, a sense of being drawn in to global problems willy-nilly, where not even the Irish coast is remote enough to escape unscathed. Although that final image — "those young faces with empty eye-sockets, up tilted and sea-gulls screaming" — is highly effective, we must wonder: have these coastal dwellers never seen drowned men before, presumably in the same ghastly condition? Why the special fuss this time? Perhaps it is the sheer number of bodies that are thus washed ashore, but the point is unclear — a very minor question about a well-written story.

The last of O'Donnell's stories, "War,"[63] should not be hastily judged by its title. Rather than being a polemic on the subject, it is a carefully developed study of peasant attitudes toward those who have fought and died — on their behalf. The story is given the same setting as *On the Edge of the Stream* and *The Big Windows* — the townland of Glenmore and village of Carrick; many of the characters from *The Big Windows* appear: we recognize Tom Manus, whose surname here is actually "Hokeys," his wife, Brigid, and his mother, Mary; also present are Briany, Sean Mor, Black Donal, Peggy, Andy the Hill, and Dan Rua, whose surname is amended to "Ruadh." Another connection is the embedded story about Briany's dog, Kruger, which is repeated with a degree of elaboration.

Six distinct sections reveal the story's tight structure. The first is introductory, where we learn about the unnamed schoolmaster, who has arranged a gathering at a local house for the purpose of discussing any possible adverse economic effects of the war between Japan and Russia (1904-05). For this purpose an itinerant "Tayman" is brought in, since he has traveled "great distances" often in his life. Because the Boer War (1899-1902) indirectly affected Ireland's economy, the locals fear that this new war may do the same.

The second section revolves around the lesson given to these backward farmers, who, uncomfortable using a globe, request the use of a flat surface — the wall — and chalk marks to show relative distances between countries. Thus are the peasants made to realize that this war is just too far away to affect them: "There's no countin' all the sheep in all the countries between us an' that fightin' if it's all land from here to there. There might as well be no war at all, for all it concerns us. The price of wool won't be touched be [sic] it. Never mind such a war."

A discussion of the glen's political past, as staunch backers of the Boers and of Parnell, constitutes the third section, and in the fourth tea is made as the people learn from The Tayman of Glenmore's reputation for its quality lime and its lively patriotic spirit.

The story takes a more serious turn in the penultimate section, which involves a discussion of the grave of a wounded fenian, who was sheltered by the peasants but died nevertheless. Since the townland values its isolation and autonomy most of all, and since it is reasonable in time of war to keep a tight lip, the fenian's grave has been left unmarked and the dead man has never been talked about since. The peasants' submerged guilt is then exposed, especially when it is remembered that, out of fear, no priest was sent for, no prayers were said, and no wake was held.

In the concluding section, the farmers file out of Tom's house, on their way to the grave site to "say the rosary over him, an' speak about him, an' be proud" of what was done for him in providing him shelter and comfort. He is to be waked "in God's house," which will finally "put things right." As it turns out, The Tayman knew the fenian, so he will speak about the dead patriot at the wake. Through talk of a war far distant from this glen, the realities of a war fought very near the townland are thereby effectively brought to light.

These three stories are satisfying pieces of fiction — certainly good enough to be included in anthologies of Irish short stories. O'Donnell's skill at rendering extremely isolated Irish rural societies, so well manifested in his novels, is clearly apparent here as well: from Kitty's accepted role in her village to the group of farmers gathered to hear about the Russo-Japanese war, the flavor of Irish community is strong. Their ignorance of world affairs is not hidden; far from it, O'Donnell exposes such ignorance in order to emphasize the greater compensation that manifests itself in neighborliness and tolerance and warmth.

Wrack

O'Donnell's dramatic output was limited to one play, *Wrack*, which ran for a full week at the Abbey in 1932 and saw a second week as a revival in 1935. For both runs the play was well-received by critics and the general public alike. Indeed, there was nothing blatant in this inoffensive little play to inspire anyone's ire. Similar in setting and circumstance to *Storm*, the play's action occurs on a highly remote Donegal island that suffers a tempestuous assault at the hands of the forces of nature. Freyer has pointed out the difficulties involved in staging, primarily attributable to the one act that takes place on the ocean at night.[64] The limitations are that nothing is seen but a lantern and nothing heard but voices, all among whatever effects of a rising storm can be reproduced. Freyer also indicates that the act was rewritten for the play's second production, without significant enough improvement. The play's five other acts present no extraordinary difficulty.

The texture of the play is actually very similar to that of the fiction: we develop the same sense that we are viewing a people, a way of life no longer extant. The Irish men and women here are living virtually the same way they have for centuries, a condition permitted and encouraged by the island's extreme isolation. That is, the channel that separates them from the Donegal coastline is not only a physical barrier but a cultural one as well. However, because of the scarcity of work, some of the islanders have been forced to travel to Scotland, a situation familiar from *Adrigoole*, and as a result a mild linguistic invasion has occurred: Scottish words, such as "the wee boat," have made their way into speech patterns and Scottish songs are admired and sung. The community is, perforce, well knit and we come to know the characters individually in a way absent from much of the drama of O'Donnell's playwright peers. Not that O'Donnell's characters all have tremendous depth to them; to the contrary, most of what we learn is as purely realistic and hence near the surface as we can expect in a work of such brevity, relative to the novels. Rarely does a character bare any of his soul to us, but we do come to know the characters' minutest quirks and most individualizing traits. There is, therefore, no strain to the dialogue and the result is that we are treated to one of the sincerest forms of realism imaginable. The surprise, of course, is that we are never bored with such faithful representation; rather, we are as amused and fascinated as we are by the best of O'Donnell's novels.

Some readers are, in fact, considerably puzzled by what they encounter in the first two acts because nothing overt "happens" in them. Character always supercedes plot, event, or situation in O'Donnell's work, even more so than in Synge's drama. In *The Playboy of the Western World* (1907) we have a "murderer" on the run; in *The Well of the Saints* (1905) we have a miracle in the offing; and in *Riders to the Sea*(1904) the audience knows a recent drowning has occurred. As great as Synge's emphasis is on character, O'Donnell's is far greater. In a society of people who are circumspect about their deepest emotions, we find instead persons like old Johnny Anthon, who is driven nearly to distraction about the customary seating arrangement when cards are played in the evening. In these close quarters, Andy Mor breathes into his ear, a situation that has given Johnny nightmares; he cannot move his seat to the position under the lamp because that is where Corney, whose eyesight is poor, must sit ; he cannot sit at the foot of the table — where Andy would not follow since he wouldn't take "his backside out of the fire to follow anybody"[65] — because then the cold would affect his legs. Concerns such as these, which are the matter of the first two acts, are presented for two basic reasons: most obviously, they serve as character development, for we come to know these folk intimately enough to care about what happens to them; secondly they develop an overwhelming sense of community, which culminates poignantly when Peter Dan and his crew are drowned while attempting to rescue Corney and his crew during the storm.

At the play's center is the Boyle family. Though Brigid and
Hughie have a number of children, we never see them and they remain mere shadows, usually reported as being watched over at
other people's houses. From a dramatic standpoint this fact is perhaps unfortunate, as the presence of children would likely bring
an added dimension to the play's pathetic final scene after Charlie
drowns. It is a curious phenomenon, since in *Islanders* O'Donnell
had already shown his capability of integrating children very effectively into the work's fabric, though we must bear in mind that
O'Donnell's greatest literary achievement, *The Big Windows*, is
similarly marked by a conspicuous absence of readily identifiable
children. Hughie himself is not particularly a well-rounded character — even some of the play's less central elderly characters are better drawn — but the few of his traits that are emphasized are strong
enough that he can by no means be considered static or flat. Most
salient early in the play is his good humor; his warm-hearted teas-
ing reveals a warmth and kindness that endear him to us as they do
to the many members of the close-knit community. He is a spiritual buoy that lifts the islanders up during the hungry, sparse
times that afflict them all. While others are prone to bickering and
despair, Hughie always maintains his equanimity and optimism.
But these charismatic aspects of his character, however effective,
are somehow not enough. The courage we sense in him towards
the end of the play sustains what we have expected of him throughout, but, although it may be argued that he is just a simple man
lacking in depth-producing complexities, we just do not see
enough of him to grant him the status of a fully rounded character.

His wife, Brigid, is, however, another matter entirely. Given the
play's relatively thorough limning of so many of this island
community's members, which thus limits the amount of dialogue
she can be allotted, she is a brilliant creation. Most important is
her overwhelming individuality, which she makes no effort to hide
or mitigate among a people who in many respects are set in their
ways because of tradition or mere habit. Where a neighbor, Mary
Jim, lives in fear that in these times of near starvation someone
may intrude during a meal and consume some precious food,
Brigid repeatedly declares her disgust for the majority of islanders
who, like Mary Jim, actually hide their food if they sense someone

approaching. It has, in fact, become a recent custom on the island
to cough loudly before arriving at a house so that food can quickly
be removed from the table. Brigid will have none of it and is
openly generous on various occasions, at the same time vigorously
assailing all the others who have let niggardliness consume their
neighborliness. In a place where all women — as in Synge's *Riders to
the Sea* — live in constant fear that the ocean may carry their men
away, Brigid is the only one who has the courage to admit that nevertheless, she "couldn't live away from it . . . bad and all as things
are" because without it she "wouldn't know how to live" (19). Despite her admirable qualities of pride and dignity, she has a sense
of resignation about her future, which she recognizes several
times as being in the hands of forces beyond her control. But what
probably endears her most to the reader is her candor. With a
wonderful sense of self-confidence, she reveals her mind to her
neighbors, to her husband, and to us. In the midst of a religiously
orthodox community she can declare that though she does pray
whenever Hughie is caught fishing during a sudden squall, it is not
the prayer itself that eases her mind, but the fact that her mind is
occupied by the *act* of praying. None of the other characters reveal
as much about themselves. Brigid's individuality is valued by her
husband, who compliments her various times because of it. This
would suggest a strong, healthy marriage, and Hughie is exactly
the easygoing kind of man who would leave Brigid all the room
she needs to grow and thereby to maintain her individuality. Indeed, there is every indication of a certain equality in their union,
coupled with warmth and tolerance, that further draws the reader
towards them. For instance, he helps Brigid with tasks traditionally reserved for women, as when he brings her tea and boxty while
she is busy drying her hair (48). On the other hand, Hughie can
chide Fanny when she pleads that her son be prevented from join-
ing the crew: "Wouldn't the whole island laugh at a man that drew
back for a woman's talk?" (55).

Fanny's fears, which extend from her first entrance on stage to
her last, define her as a character. Her misgivings are supported
during the calm before the storm by omens she sees about the island: cobwebs on the grass, cormorants on the rocks "with their
wings out," and the general lack of birds about the bay (23). These
signs presage a coming storm, which, when coupled with the des-

perate need for money and food, will put her son at great risk if herring is sighted. Fanny is, therefore, near distraction when Charlie indeed joins Peter Dan's crew, of which Hughie is a member, and when the boats go out and are caught in the sudden storm. It is understandable that she curses Corney's boat and wishes that Corney's cries for help had been smothered by the sea; then Peter Dan would not have ventured deeper into the storm to render aid, and Charlie would be alive at the play's end. Finally, she curses the sea itself, which is never satisfied. If we assume that she is a widow — a fact left unclear by the play, since her husband is never mentioned — she is obviously in many respects a counterpart to Synge's Maurya, except that at the end she feels no sense of resignation; rather, she is bitter, resentful, and nearly hysterical. It is likely that O'Donnell, surely aware of Synge's great play, felt that the latter reaction was the more realistic — and more in keeping with the coastal life he had lived, not merely visited.

The character of Mary Jim serves as the most direct foil to Brigid. We see her most clearly in the first act, a negativist who, always fearing the worst, is immediately ready to give up rather than courageously endure. When times are hard, she becomes moody to the point of exasperating the usually even-tempered Brigid. Her spiritual weakness and inertia, rather than appearing purely idiosyncratic, are intended as being representative of all island women who complain about the hardness of island life and talk about leaving, but who lack the pluck to do so.

The remaining characters are more elderly and serve primarily a comic purpose up until the storm strikes. Paddy Cormac is best remembered for his spluttering anger when some sheep escape their enclosure and eat his prized cabbages; despite evidence to the contrary, he insists on blaming his wife, Kitty, who knows full well how to handle him. She refuses to acknowledge his childish vexation and continues to knit, bringing his pride down several notches by even forcing him to help her wind the yarn. Thus is he effectively disarmed and domesticated, and the absurdity of his charges underscored. We have already seen Johnny Anthon's comic discomfiture around the card table, and he is overall the most eccentric of O'Donnell's characters in this play. His status is assured with proclamations such as that some day "some smart man somewhere will find a way to listen to herrin'" (69), since "every animal [makes] a noise of its own." But Johnny comes to symbolize a very important quality of the old guard when the immensity of the storm is beginning to be realized by all; he wants to cut the nets and see to Corney's crew's shouts for help, but his own crew, led by his son, Dan, will have none of it. Forsaking the communal values passed down through countless generations, Dan and the others instead can think only that at long last their nets are finally bursting with herring. The dialogue makes clear that, more than hunger, it is the disease of capitalist greed that is to be blamed. Corney's death then creates a nicely conceived double irony in that, though he is the most skeptical character in the play, it is he who ventures furthest into the storm; and in that, because of his carelessness, the strongest crew on the island rows to its death trying to save him — resulting in the loss of Hughie, Charlie, and Peter Dan.

Even as *Riders to the Sea* makes highly effective use of corresponding foreshadowing and dramatic irony, so too does *Wrack*. We have already noted Fanny Brian's various omens as one manifestation of these qualities. Elsewhere we are unobtrusively reminded every so often that "the sea can be sudden" (*e.g.,* 49), so that when the miraculous calm occurs, we know for certain that the storm is inevitable. The fact that Fanny was right is underscored when at the end we learn of the vision she had and kept to herself: she saw the boats, the rough waters, and then "a big coffin drifting helpless in the sea, and a sail peeling itself off a mast and winding itself round the bodies of dead men. It was Peter Dan's boat" (93).

In studying a literary work where those characters best equipped to survive adversity are the ones who fail to do so, we would be remiss if we did not consider whether the play is naturalistic or not, especially when a substantial portion of the author's fiction — most notably *Adrigoole* — can be thus categorized. It is worth mentioning here that a monumental Atlantic storm actually did strike the west coast of Ireland on October 28, 1927, just a few years before the play was written, and this is likely the chief immediate inspiration for the play. But the unleashed forces of nature alone are not enough to create the naturalistic setting; the fishermen in O'Donnell's play lose their lives also because of unfavorable social circumstances; since they are poor and live on an island that generally resists agriculture, and since herring has not been sighted in months, they are compelled to take risks. No real choice is involved in the matter. A further irony is that in all likelihood the storm was driving the herring ahead of it, as if putting bait in a trap; if we keep in mind the effects of the west wind in Shelley's poem, affecting life far below the water's surface, this hypothesis seems particularly eligible. The play also hints at another social circumstance working against the islanders: they are aware of the advantage of owning larger boats, which would not so easily be swamped, but poverty again traps them without choice because such boats simply cannot be afforded. Smaller examples of circumstances interfering in the characters' lives can be found, adding depth to the naturalistic atmosphere, rounding it out and giving it a richer texture. Perhaps the best example occurs in the middle of the third act, during the last time Hughie and Brigid are alone together — an intimate domestic moment, coming directly after they have been discussing their son, Cormac, and his likely future as boat builder. According to the stage directions, Hughie impulsively puts down his pipe and tobacco, quickly walks over to her, "puts a hand under her chin and tilts up her face" (53); he is obviously about to kiss her, the last opportunity he is to have to display his affection in private, when the customary cough of someone approaching the house is heard. Meaningfully, it is Fanny Brian, the doomsayer; circumstances have intervened and the kiss is aborted.

Social pressure also manifests itself as a naturalistic force. As is the case with Fanny Brian's misgivings about her son, the alarmed Brigid cannot prevent Hughie from going out with the crew because of the tremendous embarrassment that would result for Hughie, since, as we have already seen, women's fears are to be dismissed in macho fashion. A different social — and psychological — phenomenon occurs as a result of the poverty and hunger: people simply begin to act differently, and the result is uniformly divisive, as when a person is considered a good neighbor only if he clears his throat loudly to warn a family at meal of his impending arrival. But the differences are not always implicitly codified and can go beyond sociological change to strike at society's individual members, as when Brigid angrily complains to Mary Jim: "If it's not silence it's a spill of talk, and the silence is the same as the talk; a

cover to hide one mind from the other. Is there a house on the island with two women on the floor but there's tightness and sharp-
ness and silence? Is there a houseful of childer but they're nagging
and scratching at one another? Isn't the whole island in the fid-
gets? And what is at the root of it all? I'll tell you, it's hunger; aye, it
is, hunger." But Brigid, as is her custom, proceeds quite candidly
to personalize her criticism: "Listen to me, Mary Jim: if you come
with me to the carrigeen strand another day and carry on the way
you done this day, I'll brain you. Not a word out of you except
every now and then a wheeze of a tune as if something was dying in
you: I used to rasp my fingers on the edges of the rocks to keep
from screeching: what in God's name is wrong with you?" (both
passages: 16). Not only is poor Mary Jim suffering the island's general malaise, but one of her children is ill as well as hungry. As is
typical in naturalistic works of art, the siege of forces is varied, relentless, and conspiratorial.

Perhaps the most significant level of tension occurs when hunger and deprivation reach deepest into the spirit of these normally
selfless, community-oriented people. The most overt case comes
in the storm scene, when Corney's cries for help are flimsily ex-
plained away in the mania of hauling the rich, heavy nets aboard.
More insidious, however, is the steady sense of inertia and despair
that spreads through the islanders. Which strikes first — physical
paralysis or spiritual — is impossible to determine, for obviously
the two are interrelated: "I'm not able to hope for anything: I just
pull away. I'm that lazy now I don't want to get up. I'll be that lazy
when I go home I won't want to get out of my wet clothes. Did you
ever notice how sleepy you get when you sit at the fire in your wet
clothes? I hate to change"(17).

Mary Jim's condition is virtually a form of living death — for she
has all but lost her will to survive. Any initial suspicions on our part
are confirmed when a little later on she declares, "I'm as dead as
the sea out there" (18). Feeling "worn out" and beyond hope of
"awakening" (20), she very briefly contemplates exile, but as if she
were a character out of *Dubliners*, she is already too exhausted to
entertain the fleeting thought realistically. She is as trapped as
Eveline Hill.

Finally, we must extend our investigation to the theological
realm. Though the characters, all good Catholics, seem reasonably

devoted to their religion, there is no way for them to account for such things as their current — and, technically, sinful — sense of despair, of being abandoned, nor for how the sea virtually decimates their neighbors and loved ones. In the grips of their grief they understandably question their god's motives for ordering human events, searching for any sense of fairness. Thus, while Brigid is considering Hughie's fate, she wonders "surely, surely, if they went to help somebody God would help them" (91). Obviously not. And when the truth of Hughie's death finally begins to strike home, she can declare, "God wouldn't do that and the sea couldn't" (92); but it is painfully clear that it has happened. Her phrasing is significant here too: if the sea is incapable, then god has taken up the slack. Of course, in keeping with the play's other naturalistic features, we can see that she is simply wrong in both statements. The sea, as a naturalistic force, has just claimed a few more victims; god has nothing to do with it. For various reasons, the play is comparable to Crane's famous story, "The Open Boat," in which the character of the oiler fails to survive. In both works of art, those most likely to endure the ocean's power are the ones whose lives are immediately claimed. The sea, in each case, remains a mere force, tossing the lives of men about without method or pattern. Thus we see clearly the particular kind of naturalism that forms the basis for this play: rather than being deterministic naturalism, where there is a sense of order and fate — a plan of some sort — what we have instead is random naturalism, where each of us is, as the cliché goes, "like a feather in the wind," tossed about in completely random fashion.

As in *Riders to the Sea*, conventional religion is a failure in the face of such adversity. Other comparisons between the two plays have been mentioned throughout this chapter, but one more, of considerable significance, remains to be acknowledged. Both plays are not only naturalistic but tragic as well: Synge's involves the suffering of Maurya and the cumulative deaths of eight brave men; O'Donnell's involves the suffering of Brigid and Fanny and the deaths of the various fishermen, with special focus on Hughie's death. Synge's play is the more tragic in the Aristotelian sense, but O'Donnell's seems to inspire more pity. Part of the reason is that the ending of each play has a distinctly different sort of strong emotional impact on the reader. Some readers prefer the sparse economy of Synge's play, with its blunt stoic conclusion and Maurya's tired acceptance; but others prefer O'Donnell's in large part because of the ironic accumulation of sincere religious devotions. Charlie sprinkles himself with holy water just prior to boarding his boat (73); the act is useless. Brigid has prayed before but suddenly finds herself unable to pray (88) when the reality of Hughie's death overwhelms the faith of religion. And then we have the twice-repeated phrase, "God is stronger than the storm" (90), totally ineffective words as far as providing spiritual or emotional support — empty, meaningless. Because of these ironies, the ending of *Wrack* will seem to some more moving, more filled with pathos, especially so at the moment when all fall on their knees and begin — probably reflexively — to pray. What would seem according to the play to be a waste of time moves us *because* of its uselessness, because we know that, as Brigid has long before pointed out, the *act* of praying relieves the mind from thinking. The scene is comparable to that at the end of Frank O'Connor's "Guests of the Nation," one of the most moving pieces of Irish literature ever written. And ultimately it is the sadness we feel after having come to know people — ordinary people — like these so well that recommends the play most highly. The sociology, anthropology, and folklore interest and fascinate us; but it is our involvement with the characters as quirky individuals that enables us to be significantly moved. The term, "tragic" is surely both accurate and appropriate.

The Gates Flew Open

It has by now become manifestly obvious that as a creative artist O'Donnell conceived of things episodically. More often than not his novels take the form of a barrage — usually a highly effective barrage — of tiny chapters. His only play, *Wrack*, which is by no means an overly lengthy work, is divided into six acts. Even the short story, "War," is composed of six plainly discernible units. What we have in *The Gates Flew Open* (1932) is an autobiographical prose work that clearly does not diverge from the pattern evident in these other genres.

I would not grant to *The Gates Flew Open* the status of formal autobiography; it is more properly classified instead as a jail journal — and some parts are in fact direct quotations from O'Donnell's jail diary. I make the distinction because much of it seems too rough and unpolished — "slangy and slipshod,"[66] as Freyer points out — to qualify it as autobiography in the formal tradition of Yeats, Moore, and O'Casey. Once the distinction has been made, however, we can accord the work some praise as being a very good jail journal: entertaining, informative, and historically fascinating. And we do find among its pages the genesis of various parts of several O'Donnell novels, which lends added interest for literary scholars.

In the book's very first chapter, when O'Donnell finds himself in D Wing of Mountjoy Prison, we are reminded of Hughie Dalach, protagonist of *Adrigoole*. O'Donnell is forced into erecting self-defenses against the loneliness and near-claustrophobia suffered by an island man who has had the sky stolen from him; where O'Donnell at one point counts bolts, Hughie was depicted as scouring out the filth from between the floorboards, as if he were cleaning out the bottom of drainage ditches. One wonders, in fact, whether O'Donnell's prison experiences merely draw attention to his eye for precise detail or actually played a role in developing his skill: "Motor cars on the road with an occasional glimpse of faces; the laughter of passing men and women; the sky with showers of rain, the distant fields with moving cattle; the barking of a dog at night time; drip, drip, drip from the outside, little provocative throbs of life stirred in me."[67] This view from O'Donnell's cell window, taken from a later chapter, reminds us of the boring routine-wracked drudge of the prisoner's life; the "opportunity" to look at life very closely and to observe the smallest of details is one of the few compensations.

Often O'Donnell refers directly to his own novels. His mention of *Storm*, for instance, is quite illuminating: " I wrote the opening scene of *Storm* but after a few weeks I forgot about it all and lived in the jail fever and was of it, for the magic word "escape" rocketed into my mind and I shot up to it"(52). Through passages such as this, we gain a clear insight into why O'Donnell's work was highly episodic from the very start, and also into why *Storm*, as an author's very first creative effort, was such an uneven novel. The remarkable thing is that the novel was written at all, for it is clear that the conditions under which the author was working — physical, psychological, and emotional — were far from conducive to the writing of a well-connected, smooth-flowing novel; obviously, the novel is the modern literary form most fragile if attempted under circumstances such as those that defined this desultory part of O'Donnell's life.

We are also afforded significant glimpses into the creation of *Islanders*, O'Donnell's far superior second novel, to which O'Donnell also makes direct reference on several occasions. Its earliest pages he originally penned while in jail, where in fact he managed to create one of the novel's important scenes, the one in which "Charlie Doogan leans on a spade . . . and sees the gannet circle over the little dark patch where no cloud could be reflected" (167). And O'Donnell makes claims whose justness cannot be challenged: "I know that I know the insides of the minds of the mass of the folk in rural Ireland: my thoughts are distilled out of their lives"(167).

The depth of character with which his greatest creations are im-
bued is a testament to the truth of this admittedly self-conscious
pronouncement. This is precisely in large part why, in his best
work, we come to know the characters so well and are completely
convinced about their "rightness" as realistic creations. The deft,
comfortable way in which O'Donnell writes about them reveals a
confidence that exudes certainty. In another chapter, O'Donnell
makes a statement that at first surprises us, but whose innate truth
is soon realized: "Jail life reminded me vividly of the few years I
had spent on small islands. You leaned your shoulder against the
cell door and looked out wondering whether you would go here
for cards, or there for chess, or somewhere else for discussion.
And just as the best oarsman, the crack helmsman, the melodeon
player, the damnedest liar, stood out as personalities in an island
community, so did individuals emerge in prison and become the
coloured threads of its passing days"(28).

Albeit in a limited way, we can piece together aspects of
O'Donnell's creative process from passages such as these, especially as they illuminate his ability to realize, envision, and then create convincing characters. The identification of individual quirks
of character seems to be a highly developed natural skill in
O'Donnell, a skill that is, of course, connected to the love and understanding of his people that pervade his work.

In his thirty-sixth chapter, O'Donnell gives us the germ of what
was to become his great seriocomic novel, *On the Edge of the Stream*,
which was published two years after *The Gates Flew Open*.
O'Donnell's train of thought leading to his reflections on the cooperative movement in Ireland is precipitated by his confrontation with a young brat of a prisoner, in which, "all eyes and hair,
you see the spirit of Masonry, Hibernianism, and their kindred in-
sincerities" (208). What has offended O'Donnell particularly here
is the boy's ostentatious and mindless display of piety, an action
that takes O'Donnell back to his own boyhood, when the co-opera-
tive "captured [his] imagination" but was immediately attacked by
an "opposition [that] fought bitterly under religious slogans."
O'Donnell then goes on to declare his angry frustration at the use
of "religious slogans in political and social struggles," which have
hurt him "by their terrible dishonesty" (208). These are the very
frustrations faced by Daniel Corkery's characters in his theologi-

cally tactful book of largely propagandistic short stories, *The Hounds of Banba* (1920), and later by Phil Timony in O'Donnell's *On the Edge of the Stream*. In O'Donnell's book, the alliance between the established, price-gouging shopkeepers and the clergy — both of whom wanted for selfish reasons to maintain the *status quo* — was formidable but not incapable of defeat at the hands of a courageous and sincere minority of good people with farsighted vision. It should be mentioned that on the one occasion when O'Donnell recalls a priest speaking in favor of the co-op, the vast majority of the parishioners were able to dismiss his words solely on the basis of the priest's "tobacco-stained teeth," for they had never before known priests to use tobacco in any form (209). The sheepish refusal of the people to exercise their intellects and instead to follow the reflexively conservative preachings of most of the clergy — who, by rights, should not be meddling in such secular matters — inspired tremendous wrath in O'Donnell, whose response to his pious young fellow-prisoner is to "break into violent, unreasonable abuse" (208). Unreason seems to be a perfectly understandable reaction to unreason; at least temporarily it permits heartfelt frustrations to be vented.

References to other literary figures and works give some indication of O'Donnell's education and upbringing. In one instance he recalls the first book he ever read — an illustrated version of Defoe's *Robinson Crusoe* that he read with his father. O'Donnell also mentions Victor Hugo, Stevenson, Dumas, Shelley, Burns, Dickens, and Wodehouse. At one point he admits to stealing a volume of Shakespeare's plays from the officers' toilet; despite slitting the book into sections in order better to conceal it from the warders, O'Donnell is unable to prevent its eventual discovery and confiscation — a significant loss of solace for him. Elsewhere, O'Donnell mentions a nice pun on *The Book of Kells;* a collection of stories and essays written by the prisoners in Mountjoy is cleverly dubbed *The Book of Cells*. As for his contact with other literary-political figures, Ernest O'Malley is discussed (200) and later on O'Donnell expresses his regret at the recent political stance of George Russell (AE), who was now allied with the *Times* and *Independent* in opposing the Republican position relative to the Treatyites. He sees Russell as being no longer "among the gods" with his "poet's soul," and instead as having descended and become "an old man up on the jail chimney-pots making his own thunder" (217).

O'Donnell's contempt for a meddling clergy and for those who mouthe pieties as a cover for their own selfish interests extends far beyond the situation involved in establishing Irish cooperatives. We must recall that strong scene in *The Knife*, where Republicans disrupt the saying of the Mass because a priest is using his pulpit to further his own highly orthodox political agenda. The likely source for O'Donnell's bitterest feelings toward the clergy is "a sleeky fat, self-satisfied" priest, whose "tuber-like, bulbous" body — with its "very fat neck and streams of sweat" (155) — provides a truly hateful correlative for his character. Speaking to his literally captive prison audience, this priest enrages the inmates to the point where they feel compelled to leave Mass. O'Donnell contemplates the negative effects of such priests on the people's idealism:

> I could only see this foul man exploding in puffs of stink, clouding the tabernacle with his stink, smothering the poor State Tommies with his stink. What chance had these men whom I knew so well to escape these puffs of stink; to them it would be as the incense at Benediction. And I saw thousands of altars all over Ireland buried in the vapours of minds like this: thousands of chapels full of this poison with hundreds of thousands of minds unprotected against its blight. What chance had we against this? The sense of being overwhelmed and buried beyond all chance of being understood soused me almost insensible. (155-56)

It is little wonder that O'Donnell, barely able to control his anger, is the first to leave, followed by most of his equally dismayed fellow prisoners. During much of the sermon, the priest in fact blatantly focuses on O'Donnell; clearly the clergy knew who he was, so that when *The Knife* was published the clergy were ready to condemn him, which indeed they did. In fact, according to O'Donnell one priest shut the doors of a hall where a meeting was to be held — only because one of the speakers was to have been "the damned man who wrote *The Knife*" (48). Part of the clerical objection had been that priests in the novel were sometimes mentioned with relatively mild expletives attached to their names by irate Republican soldiers; O'Donnell later wryly comments that ordinarily he and his fellow Republican inmates would be "aghast if a priest [were] called a son of a bitch . . . and yet . . . outbursts that carried the description of this bishop or that who was figuring in the day's news made such a phrase almost respectful" (48). O'Donnell does, however, seem at some pains to show that these attitudes were directed solely at such priests who crossed the line into politics. Regarding that priest who most negatively inspired him, O'Donnell makes sure to point out that otherwise "relations between the clergy and prisoners . . . were quite cordial" at Finner Camp, though this could not be said of what he had previously experienced at Mountjoy (154). The strongest counterbalancing image of the clergy comes late in the book, in this case "a fine trio of priests" whom O'Donnell fondly recalls by name. Actually one of them had distinct political leanings, but Father Troy presented O'Donnell no problems because he was "in sympathy with [the Republicans] in [their] struggle and he didn't go behind the door to say it" (207). Reading between the lines, however, one senses an O'Donnell counting his blessings while digging his fingernails into his palms when it comes to dealing with the clergy. By far the bulk of his specific commentary is negative, though this is not surprising coming from a man who is making an effort to promote change in a stubborn land that understandably remains highly orthodox and suspicious, especially when its religious leaders are involved.

Those who might read *The Gates Flew Open* as a means of exploring what prison life was actually like during this period of Irish history with its shifting allegiances will not be disappointed. As might be expected, much of the book is exactly a detailed recounting of O'Donnell's prison experience, which he presents in large part as typical, save that as a "member of the I.R.A. executive" (25) he was at times treated more severely than the average Republican detainee. Still, quite a few were executed, a fate that he apparently escaped only narrowly.

The most thoroughly described accounts are restricted to the book's first ten chapters. This is perhaps why as a connected narrative *The Gates Flew Open* becomes much more interesting later on, after his transfer to Tintown; the early chapters seem somewhat disconnected and hold little interest except as relatively autonomous bits of information about prison life. The early Mountjoy sections also assume a bit too much — that we will recognize certain people's names and some slang terms, for instance. But details about a prison revolt, the ensuing discussions with prison leaders, and the aftermath are clearly conveyed. Prevalent is a sense that the prisoners are more in control of the prison interior than are the guards. Tunnels are dug, escape attempts seem almost routine (though not all are successful), and warders are manipulated. In one humorous episode, this manipulation reaches its zenith when we find the prison commandant, nicknamed "Paudeen," unwittingly leading the way for a group of prisoners, O'Donnell among them, to steal wood for use in making shelves for individual cells (chapter ten). Earlier (chapter four), O'Donnell has explicitly described the process by which any heavy door may be incapacitated and effectively prevented from being locked: "The only weapon required is a book. If the book is too thick, slit off some of the pages. The only book in my cell was a Bible and I had to slit it in two. Insert the book, whole or in part, between the door and the case right close to the hinge and then slam the door. The doors are very heavy and they normally fit closely into their steel frames but now the impact against the book stretches the hinge spring and the door overlaps the casing. To remedy this strain is a big job; the whole door must be taken down and new hinges fitted "(24).

Thus it is that virtually no part of the prison is off limits to the inmates, as cell doors are rendered inoperable faster than they can be repaired or replaced. O'Donnell's pragmatic approach to the use of his Bible is consistent with his overall view of his religion. It is our basic goodness as human beings and our love of Christ that matters most; technicalities imposed by mere mortals — even those residing in Rome — matter little. In this case, respect for paper and print is eclipsed by the exigencies of men seeking to promote their own freedom from oppressive forces.

Interestingly enough, once *The Gates Flew Open* moves beyond these initial chapters, not only does the narrative become more readable and engrossing, but its actual historical context finally begins to become more than passingly relevant. As Freyer has accurately observed, O'Donnell's book is one of "the relatively few primary sources for anyone wishing to study the political history of the period."[68] The executions initiated by the Free State government began in 1922 with the death of Erskine Childers, accused of treason; in the prisons the psychological and emotional effects were severe, especially since the inmates' anger and dismay gave birth to a tremendous desire for vengeance, but their impotence to exact any revenge was painfully obvious. From O'Donnell's perspective, the succeeding executions became infinitely more personal with the deaths of four close friends — shot in reprisal for the killing of a Free State politician. The mounting strain is recorded by O'Donnell: the prison wing becomes "a grave" as the men become "a wordless, soulless movement of lives suddenly empty" (86); O'Donnell feels that his six months in prison "stretch in a grey, dull waste to the edge of the years that had been so alive" (89). In general, O'Donnell's diction in these dark chapters clearly and directly indicates the spiritual living death descending on the jailed Republicans, but an even better indirect indicator of the hardening of heart being experienced by O'Donnell and his comrades is his casual use of highly charged ordinary words — such as "batch" (90) in reference to the next series of executions. The extent of O'Donnell's proximity to death can be seen when he tells us that "it was an easy atmosphere to die in, for . . . living had no special call just then" (90). For a while, however, spirits are rejuvenated: the moment marking the end of the war — and of the executions — occurs in the book when a fellow prisoner, with "his hat off and his face . . . shining" (171), reads the account printed in the *Irish Independent*; and when the Treaty party "wins" the ensuing election by only the tiniest of majorities, Republican spirits are uplifted by the realization that their cause is not dead in the hearts of the general population — and, immediately, healthy activity begins once again with the construction of a brand-new escape tunnel.

But, of course, these were unsettled times and a return to spiritual darkness was inevitable. "The Free State Tommies" at Arbour Hill Military Detention Barracks continued to mistreat prisoners (chapter 33), for example, but probably the biggest single postwar setback was the failure of the forty-one day hunger strike, initiated in an effort to rally public support for the Republican cause and ultimately to win unconditional release for those imprisoned for political reasons. At first highly visible and successful — with crowds singing their solidarity outside Kilmainham to the point where

O'Donnell is emotionally moved — the hunger strike eventually began to break down as public support leveled off. O'Donnell records the various stages of suffering resulting from his self-imposed famine, such as seeing stars with any sudden movement (215, 218); intense headaches (223); uncontrollable itching (223); and numbness in the hands (224). Finally, when defectors became too numerous and some deaths began to occur among the faithful, the strike broke down entirely and was officially cancelled — a tremendous disappointment and effectively a failure. This is the last major movement of *The Gates Flew Open*.

Freyer has written that O'Donnell was "the most literate" among Republican leaders, "so his testimony has documentary value for the historian."[69] This is quite true, but because of O'Donnell's artistic talent as a writer we receive added perspective by way of several moments of significant personal revelation. We have already seen some of these moments — his first day in prison, his feeling of "soullessness" during the period of executions. The twenty-fifth chapter explains how he kept himself sane during his five months' stretch of solitary confinement in Finner Camp; constantly aware that he is a hostage liable to be executed at any given moment, he occupies his body by doing calisthenics and his mind by "keeping it empty of vital thoughts" (138). In another case, he is visited in his cell by several former I.R.A. officers, now loyal Free Staters. The chat is at first easygoing, but soon becomes uncomfortable: "In the midst of our talk an awkwardness developed: it came suddenly and we were all aware of it without being aware of its origin: none of us had said anything to cause it, but suddenly the whole situation was unreal. Why should I be in here with these lads my jailers? I found I was staring at them and they at me. I sat up in bed rising slowly like a man raising his head to a sound and they got up on their feet and went out. I heard a man blow his nose in the corridor and when I lay down I found there were tears in my eyes "(160).

O'Donnell's emotional response, coming as it does after a moment of clear revelation, is handled in the same manner as it is in his creative work — striking us as genuine and heartfelt and realistic. One early such situation, whose correlating stimulus is far more immediately intense, is remembered by O'Donnell on many occasions long after its frightening occurrence: while alone and digging a long and narrow escape tunnel deep underground, O'Donnell is veritably buried alive during a sudden cave-in. Thus held in place, unable to retreat and hardly able to breathe, he is forced to discipline his terrified mind and hold on until after considerable time someone discovers him and helps pull him back and then out, physically unhurt but psychologically greatly affected (109-11). In later moments of great stress or when he is feeling emotionally or spiritually claustrophobic, he recalls this experience and draws strength from it. It proves a highly effective barrier against despair in crucial situations.

Perhaps most highly revealing is the section on O'Donnell's perceptions during the hunger strike. At the beginning of the thirty-seventh chapter, he declares that "the greatest sensation of a hunger strike is the exhilaration the mind achieves; it becomes so lit up that you cannot but be aware of its blaze and brilliance. Mine seemed to rustle like flames that sweep the approaches to new thought with unblinking clarity" (210). To many of us it will appear surprising that such effects would occur due to hunger, when the reverse might be most likely expected: a kind of thick mental stoppage leading to stupor. But O'Donnell goes even further by claiming that not only his present circumstances but even past occurrences are seen in a new, deeply insightful light that he describes as "cold, uncompromising . . . and sympathetic" (210). Successfully conveyed in this chapter's relatively abstract content is the sense of the peeling away of the layers of ordinary reality so that a certain level approaching, if not attaining, the level of mysticism is reached: "Life was revealed in new beauty; I knew that life had not been [fully] lived; that there are qualities in our nature that are never stirred, that we thin our lives down and starve in a world of riches" (211). The final irony at the end of the passage is surely conscious. Throughout these pages — which detail a process of psychological, emotional, and even spiritual purification — the ironic equation is developed that the more O'Donnell is denied physical sustenance the greater his access to life's submerged spiritual realities, something like a monkish asceticism except significantly bereft of conventional religious overtones. It is also interesting that the only negative mental effect of his hunger is what he calls "the apprehension of death" (220).We have already discussed the negative physical effects, which, because of their intense nature, are surprisingly relegated to a secondary position relative to what becomes a dominating psychological condition, not an ordinary, easily understood fear of death but a pervasive, shadowy sense that control can be wrested at any moment from the mind and overpowered by the starved vessel that contains the mind — vulnerability given access by the weakest variable in the equation. That sense of vulnerability and unpredictability was horrifying to him.

After the hunger strike was called off and he had, apparently, fully recovered, O'Donnell made his well-known escape in March of 1924, after twenty-one total months of imprisonment. Disguising himself with various articles of clothing, O'Donnell simply — and courageously — walked up to the gates that, as if by miracle, were flung open for him. Equally mysterious was the fact that the searchlight was not operational that night, and it would appear that the guards at each gate, failing to see his face clearly enough, merely assumed he was someone else and accommodated the figure that walked toward them with such ease and authority. It was an idea whose boldness, combined with sheer luck, made effective.

The Gates Flew Open is by no means great literature in the tradition of *Hail and Farewell*, but it holds our attention firmly enough to make its reading worth our while. Its historical value, in fact, surely outweighs its literary worth, for it is a unique document in the insights it affords us into this turbulent period in Irish history and politics. This does not mean that the deeply personal insights the book reveals to us are not significant enough; they are. Rather, it is the infrequency of such insights coupled with some very rough and slangy prose, that will probably disappoint some readers, especially those whose interest in historical matter is minimal. Still, if we measure *The Gates Flew Open* by what we have learned after reading it, most of us will be satisfied.

Salud! An Irishman in Spain

Five years later, O'Donnell published his next autobiographical tome, *Salud! An Irishman in Spain*, which records O'Donnell's experiences during the Spanish Civil War. O'Donnell was already in Spain when the fighting broke out, not out of anticipation to help his Spanish anti-fascist comrades, but by sheer luck, for he had merely joined some Irish friends who sought out a warm climate for their vacation. Part of the reason for his making the trip was that he needed a holiday from Ireland — especially from the oppression of the Irish Catholic establishment. Desiring a place "where they have no religion,"[70] O'Donnell at first considered Scotland but instead opted for Spain, probably because though the people's devotion to their religion was strong, clerical power was nowhere near as absolute as it often appeared to O'Donnell in Ireland. The other part of O'Donnell's reason to travel was to find a quiet, stable environment where he could "finish some work that was crumbling in [his] mind from neglect" (7). On 2 July, 1936, O'Donnell arrived in Barcelona, but it was not long before he had to abandon any creative efforts he had planned to make and found himself instead suddenly thrust by circumstances into a war zone.

Freyer has observed that the book was "hastily composed"[71] and there is much in *Salud!* that supports such an observation. Though the chapters are in many instances substantially longer than those in *The Gates Flew Open*, the book is nevertheless highly episodic, as we have virtually come to expect from O'Donnell; sometimes it is difficult to tell what principle, if any, holds a chapter together as a unit. In fact, the longer chapters often seem arbitrary collections of series of events — as if he were trying to tie together tiny chapters of his customary length, such as those in *The Gates Flew Open*. And towards the end the chapters generally tend to become far shorter, as if O'Donnell were exhausting his creative energy — a hypothesis supported by the fact that the book does not so much conclude as peter out. Certainly there is no real sense of closure. Some readers will recognize this general pattern from *Adrigoole* — as if O'Donnell, man of action, were running out of patience with the necessarily stationary requirements of producing quality creative writing. Other places where the writing will dissatisfy most readers are those where O'Donnell frequently reduces his narrative to political, historical, sociological, or economic lecturing — for several pages at a time. Also unfortunate is his philosophizing, as when he ponders the causes of war (45-6). Perhaps the least engaging part of the book comes in the twelfth chapter, in which O'Donnell attends a meeting of the Anarchist Farmers' Congress. Most of it reads like the meeting's minutes; for instance, three consecutive paragraph openings read "Bellmunt said," "Banolas said," and "Sabadell suggested" (168-69).

However, I am glad to say that despite such serious drawbacks, sudden brilliances are not uncommon. For instance, O'Donnell frequently captures not only the fervor of idealism but the accompanying clear-sighted reality that is inextricably a part of the picture: "But heat, dust, mosquitoes, flies, can make a man look up and notice the sun. I remember noticing we were columns of dust sweeping through dust, wearing dust-masks, and when, for no reason in the world, we opened our mouths to roar, sand stuffed our throats like grain in a hopper! Villages appeared in the dust, bulking up suddenly like ships in a fog, and you heard noise and knew people were cheering, and you cheered"(106).

The heavy emphasis on the dust is not only realistic but also symbolic, for many of these men were on their way to Saragossa to be massacred, a fact of which O'Donnell was surely aware while writing in retrospect. But primarily O'Donnell is concerned with showing how things really were — men buoyed by their enthusiasm but virtually unable to breathe because of the dust of reality. O'Donnell's capacity for rendering camera-eye realism has always been strong, especially in such novels as *Islanders* and *The Big Windows*; in *Salud!* O'Donnell does not shy away from his obligations

as a realist writing in a wartime setting. During an air raid,
O'Donnell witnesses among the "pandemonium" a piercing
screeching sound and soon discovers its source:

> A girl swung round the corner and came into clear view. One
> side of her face was blood dark, and black spots showered down
> her grey-white frock. . . . The screech snapped, an abrupt break
> like that of a steam-whistle, only cleaner. The screech seemed to
> stand by itself in the air for a second . . . and then . . . she let go,
> folding inwards as though her body would leave itself ready to
> be put away. . . . When the dead are gathered together what is an
> air raid but a few bodies — a child, a girl, a man, a grandfather, a
> leg, cuts, tears . . . [a] conflict of voices clawing at one another:
> men and women with all the lights of reason gone out. (204-05)

Machine-gun fire is presented with equal effectiveness: "They ran
into a sheet of lead that cut through their bodies so solidly that
they halted sharply as if impaled before the crackling machine-
guns. They fell slowly in the clear light with grotesque tiny movements; you never saw such tiny flips of limb tell such a story" (206).
If we consider that O'Donnell had witnessed incidents at least
equally horrifying during the Irish Civil War, we can gain a measure of his capacity to feel, for clearly he has not become inured to
human suffering and the grotesqueries of war. O'Donnell's eye
for detail, however, extends far beyond graphic scenes such as
these and reveals to us once again his understanding of ordinary
village folk. Reading the subtlest of signs in villager behavior, he
sees how the men put their hearts into their ploughing, while
women "moved around . . . and talked, and put their heads together in the dark way women will when the news lies heavily on
the mind" (146). His capacity for insight into human nature is also
evident, as we can see in this commentary on the Fascist massacre
at Badajos and its eventually parabolic effect on government
troops the more the story is told: ultimately "it became publicity
for the other side. There comes a stage when atrocity stories do
not rouse courage but start panic; it depends on the telling, and
some publicity splashes the horrors of events to such a degree, that
the horror of it all acts like the sniff of blood to cattle penned near
a slaughterhouse" (201). But O'Donnell's strongest descriptive talent rises to the surface in occasional portraits that have an air of

rightness, of authenticity — and universality — about them, as in this example about a man whose response to the difficult times in which he finds himself is to work correspondingly harder: "Look at the set of that man out there in the field, lean and tough in the neck like a peak, thick in the thighs like the trees. . . . But for all that he growls, this slave of the fields really takes the scarcity as the un-alterable way of nature, and seeks to remedy the hardship by harder work, more frugal living. Dumb, dark, sturdy man out there in the sun, eyes dark with the soil. Water and green leisure are dim even in dreams" (183, 184). The poor farmer's response is all too understandable, for O'Donnell sees that despite the man's good soul, he is a victim of modern economics — the unwitting dupe of a system that creates anger and then absorbs that anger to its own benefit. Working harder is more of a way for him to vent his frustrations, giving him the impression that something must be being gained when nothing actually is. O'Donnell's socialism is ev-ident not only through his choice of subject here, but also in his diction and tone.

O'Donnell's grasp of the universal is especially noteworthy in *Salud!*, where we are made to recognize human types even as O'Donnell limns individuals. The following sketch of father and son is particularly adept in its economy of words: "Youths with arms attracted new attention. Here and there goodbyes were being said. I saw and heard a lame man say goodbye to his son. The lad who was going was bursting with pride and impatience, and the father was aglow with pride in his boy. The populace . . . felt their youth to be carrying the passion of those hours" (102). Once the suggestion has been made, our own imaginations contribute the rest that rounds out the picture. We know it is a scene that has occurred millions of times in virtually every culture and era in human history. O'Donnell makes clear this universal outlook early in the book when he declares that the central purpose of *Salud!* is to show that "Spaniards are like the rest of us, brave and cowardly by turns, gentle and savage, dumb, bewildered, and splendid as human nature itself. And human nature is as constant as the tides" (9). The sense of neighborliness that pervades O'Donnell's fiction and drama also becomes a universal quality, for "After all one fish-ing village should be as neighbourly as another; could anything be obscure in the lives of folk who wrestled the sea for their living anywhere?" (7-8). Indeed O'Donnell frequently sees his Ireland reflected in Spanish scenes. We understand O'Donnell's regret, for instance, that primitive village life and values are eroding in Spain as they are in Ireland: "You got the feeling that this world of fisherfolk was encased in a tightening frame of promenades, hotels, pensions and imitation casinos. The boats would soon be little more than the spinning-wheels preserved for tourists in Gaelic-speaking districts in Ireland. . . . I hate to see spinning-wheels, thatched cottages, small farms and handicraft kept alive to make a show. A fishing-village carefully preserved within a holiday resort appalls me as only exhausted forms can appall" (22). Here O'Donnell is clearly rejecting the bastardized version of Western Ireland whose purer form once inspired Yeats and Synge; instead, he is articulating a view often associated with the far more conservative Seumas O'Kelly and Daniel Corkery, who saw this repulsive trend developing over twenty years earlier and depicted it in their fiction.

But Spain was O'Donnell's declared object to be rendered and his specific observations range broadly in nature and scope. One major difference he notes between Ireland and Spain, for example, is that "Spanish Catholics do not seem to regard the Church with any of the awe so marked in Ireland" (23) since "Spain ha[s] overcome the influence of priests" (36). In part this was what allowed so many churches to be sacked by the Communists with so little public outcry; the clerical tentacles did not nearly have so strong a grip on, or as extensive an intertwining with, the Spanish people. This more relaxed relationship is perhaps best characterized in the book when O'Donnell asserts that, in Spain, "God is . . . neighbourly" (24). These are the two things O'Donnell valued most highly — God and neighborliness.

The two nations' Catholicism did bind them together in myriad ways — that is obvious. But O'Donnell himself seemed surprised when he learned of Spain's high level of sympathy for the Irish during the Troubles, especially among the Catalonians. Clashes with police outside the British Consulate had been, in fact, almost daily occurrences, and O'Donnell also reports that the death of one Irish politician during a hunger strike "provoked an uproar in Barcelona such as even Dublin itself did not surpass" (30). O'Donnell seems to trust his sources implicitly throughout *Salud!*, but at times one may wonder if O'Donnell were sometimes — amid the fervid atmosphere of idealistic zeal — merely being told what he wanted to hear. But given O'Donnell's knowledge of human nature, his experiences in dangerous situations where he knew exactly whom he could trust, and his innate wily intelligence, it is more than likely that we can put full stock in virtually all that he reports as facts obtained by way of trusted contacts.

There are times when what O'Donnell reports about Catalonian customs or social norms is merely puzzling to him. Perhaps the strangest and most striking case concerns the macho attitude of the Catalan Popular Forces, who refuse to take cover from air raids or machine-gun fire even if such life-preserving cover is close at hand. O'Donnell is clearly flabbergasted when he sees these men refusing even to fall on the ground as a minimal means of protecting themselves. Even touring foreigners became indirectly involved when their "Spanish guides would walk recklessly in the open although perfectly good cover was temptingly near" (111). And if one local militia could be convinced that the risks taken were utterly "stupid," O'Donnell would encounter the same behavior time and again in sector after sector.

What O'Donnell documents best, however, is the frequently severe confusion behind the anti-fascist lines during the war. Amply detailed is the jockeying among a motley array of different groups with at times strikingly dissimilar philosophies: Communists, Trotskyites, Socialist trade unions, Anarchists, Liberals, and the Government — among others. At one point, well after the start of hostilities, O'Donnell can report in tired tones that "the front was in the same old confusion. There was no cooperation between the commands over the various armies representing independent organizations" (155). With this much disharmony from the start, the confusion could only worsen at the municipal level. Barcelona, the primary site of O'Donnell's observations, is offered as example but with the implication that what happened there was typical — an excess of government, whereby an intricate network of frequently conflicting committees attempted to provide order. In many instances self-important little potentates could block the issue of important documents — such as travel passes — and often it was merely a case of knowing who could most effectively introduce one to influential committee members. On the streets life was often dangerous, not yet because Franco's troops were storming through them, but because "mistakes" were not infrequent; in one instance two legitimate soldiers are shot as looters, their deaths coming even as they futilely tried to explain who they were (118). A comment, made by O'Donnell in the same tired-sounding tone as before, is quite telling: "Queer, tangled old Barcelona, knitting together its new life" (125). Of course, if we pursue the path of chaos down to the level of the rural village, the trend continues. When O'Donnell's "adopted" fishing community first begins mobilization, O'Donnell can only bemusedly throw up his hands and declare, "Pandemonium. The village a bedlam of car sirens and screeching brakes. . . . Men rushed off helter-skelter. Those with nowhere to go milled around and cheered" (64, 65).

Finally, it should be noted that the Government, such as it was, only contributed to the mayhem. While ironically using stories of Fascist atrocities to inspire its soldiers, it was committing atrocities itself, especially against people who were anywhere above middle-class status or who were anti-labor in their political and philosophical sympathies. Using the war as an excuse to "track down" such arbitrarily selected victims, the militias abused their power and did nothing to promote stability and security. O'Donnell's other major complaint against the Government is its policy of looting churches, one incident of which O'Donnell himself witnessed: "The effect of the attack was also against the interests of the anti-Fascist struggle in the village, as witness the silence of the great throng which, until now, had cheered every new step taken. A steadily mounting rage was my main reaction though I could not be quite sure whether my temper drew its heat from revolt against the dark backwardness of what was taking place or from alarm at the bewilderment which such outrages must cause among Catholic masses who are sincerely anti-Fascist"(72). The resulting loss of popular support pained O'Donnell, who, as an outsider, was in better position to estimate the irreparable damage such mindless acts caused in the long run.

It is interesting how much we learn about Ireland while we are learning about Spain. Irish public opinion was pro-Fascist because the Government forces — Communists, anyway — were hated once tales of looted churches reached the home country. To exacerbate matters, incredible stories were circulated — and believed — in Ireland, including a particularly grotesque one that appeared in the newspapers about the coffins of monks and nuns being disinterred and the bodies exhumed and displayed in the streets. The effect of such reports was predictable in Ireland and in fact prompted the creation of the pro-Franco Irish Brigade under General Owen O'Duffy. A reaction then set in that led to a flow of Irishmen enlisting in the effort against the Fascists. Freyer states the obvious when he sees "an echo of the tug-of-war in Ireland between the IRA and the Republican government."[72] Also worth mentioning is O'Donnell's disgust upon returning temporarily to Ireland only to find anti-communist gangs operating under the banner of "Catholic Action." This pervasive harassment of O'Donnell and other Republicans bears all the destructive marks of McCarthyism and with its center located in the Catholic Church is dubbed "clerical tyranny" (138) by O'Donnell.

Perhaps what is most valuable in this book is what was most valuable about *The Gates Flew Open*, what it tells us about O'Donnell himself. Regarding the church-looting incident, O'Donnell makes a simple announcement that is actually the most emblematic statement I have seen him make on the subject of the Catholic Church: "I still felt that I should probably always regret that I did not attempt to get at the good sense of that Catalan crowd to end the attack on the church, though I shall always be glad to have been there when the attack was made" (77). There is no follow-up statement, so that these words are left ringing in our consciousness; if one were reading quickly, one might not even notice them or the message they carry — that on some emotional plane, O'Donnell is "glad" to have witnessed this anti-Catholic destruction. Could it be that the experience had a cathartic effect for all the cumulative frustration O'Donnell had been amassing inside him, frustration at clerical interference in the political and social realm? It is an interesting question to ponder.

As we have seen several times before, O'Donnell was a religious man when it came to heartfelt devotion. In another incident O'Donnell without much fuss shows his gallantry as well as his respect for religion when he defends a young girl's right to possess a crucifix that a guard has snatched from around her neck (151-52). As risky as the situation is, O'Donnell impulsively argues with the irate guard that she has every right to own and display it; he then returns it to her when, luckily for O'Donnell, the guard gives in.

Other examples of O'Donnell standing up for his principles are occasionally evident, perhaps most memorably when he visits Anarchist headquarters in Barcelona. There he finds a "Press Bureau" where news bulletins are being translated for transmission to France and Germany. Since nothing is being translated into English, the Government version of the war is not making its way to Britain and Ireland, and O'Donnell decides then and there to pitch in himself — after he has shown his revolutionary credentials, of course. Another case worthy of brief mention is the time O'Donnell accompanied a column on its march to the Aragon front; we have already seen his observations on the profusion of dust and high spirits that he encountered.

These parts of *Salud!* are thoroughly engaging and surely we can only regret that they do not occur more frequently. If we take them together with O'Donnell's fine portraits and sketches and his insightful observations, we can accord the status of autobiography to *Salud!* where we could not to *The Gates Flew Open*. It is not great autobiography — primarily because of the lecturing that intermittently bogs down long stretches at a time—but it seems to me nevertheless superior to *The Gates Flew Open*, despite its hasty composition. Its narrative is better sustained, more detailed, and hence more consistently engaging. It is clearly still worth reading.

There Will Be Another Day

The third and final autobiographical book in O'Donnell's canon, *There Will Be Another Day* (1963), presents the literary scholar with a number of problems, beginning with definition, or generic classification. What kind of a book is this? As we have seen in the preceding two chapters of this study, O'Donnell writes idiosyncratically along the borders of formal autobiography, with *Salud!* qualifying but *The Gates Flew Open* falling short. It seems to me that *There Will Be Another Day* also falls short, but for different reasons. McInerney, the most supportive of O'Donnell's critics, can bring himself only as far as to call it "a virtual autobiography."[73] Peter Costello all but dismisses the book, referring to it in passing as merely "some memoirs,"[74] and even O'Donnell himself, in his introduction, calls it "a booklet,"[75] though this is perhaps out of modesty. My point here is that the book is just too slight to qualify. Of course, sheer length is by no means the sole standard by which the work is being judged; rather, its brevity is one of several contributing factors affecting final classification.

There Will Be Another Day records events that took place mostly in Donegal during the land annuity agitation — from 1926 to 1932, though really O'Donnell frequently ranges back in time to cover events that took place when *The Gates Flew Open* ended in 1924 and even earlier. In his introduction, O'Donnell describes his method in writing *There Will Be Another Day*: "I would chase along country roads for a few weeks and gather the story, life-living, from the lips of those who lived it. Every now and then I made a false start, and wrote bits of notes in this townland and that, which I proposed to fit into a framework of time later, by checking them against the files of *An Phoblacht*. I had no sense of urgency about the work until Phil McCauley, secretary to the most important of all the committees, died suddenly" (5). Such a desultory method of composition must — at this relatively late stage of his life, seventy years of age — have suited him quite comfortably. However, there was still pressure on him; now it was no longer the interruptions of war, imprisonment, or activism— but the race to reconstruct the past while its witnesses were still among the living. Besides the spasmodic composing process so familiar to him, O'Donnell had other reasons to glow while creating "the book [he] always said he most enjoyed writing,"[76] according to Freyer. If this was "the most exhilarating period in Peadar O'Donnell's life, a campaign vigorously and joyfully fought in which he was indisputably the principal actor,"[77] then his pleasure in piecing events together, visiting old friends and enemies, and reliving his former political successes is quite understandable.

The central drawback to establishing *There Will Be Another Day* as real autobiography in the formal sense is that O'Donnell's tendency to lecture, a relatively minor flaw in *Salud!*, dominates the overall tenor of this book. Though its appeal is various, it is chiefly to be regarded as a history book, written by the person who lived through the events described, brought many of those events into being, and is therefore best qualified to record them. Because the book is actually a hybrid, it is clearly not just a history book, but O'Donnell's assessment of political, social, and legal matters — along with a flood of historically accurate details — prompts one to regard it as such. Frequently material is presented virtually in the form of lessons, though sometimes this is necessary so that O'Donnell's readers can have a full idea of why certain facts, acts, or anecdotes are meaningful. At other times, however, the barrage of information can be of sustained interest only for the specialist historian or perhaps biographer.

One instance where a historical lesson is warranted is among the opening pages, which constitute a survey of Irish politics and history leading up to the "land annuity agitation."[78] Along the way, O'Donnell explains how "land annuity" (20-21) is a form of extortion on the part of the British that was enforced by Irishmen upon one another; he also details the results of withholding rents as a part of the agitation; as the arrears mounted up it meant ruin for the majority of small landholders and renters who could not pay the aggregate lump sum (22-23). This situation "legally" called for the seizing of cattle by bailiffs, resulting in what amounted to a smaller-scale return to the outrageous agrarian policies of the later nineteenth century. In response, O'Donnell promoted peaceful resistance, and explains a few of the methods he used: "The bailiff would run into clods and sods and angry dogs; not even the guards would expect people to ask him in for tea. It was no part of the guards' duty to help the bailiff get stampeded cattle back on the road. If the bailiff brought a lorry, to get the cattle away quickly, I did not know whose duty it would be to remove the scatterment of stones on the public road that prevented the lorry from getting past. . . . But no matter who removed the stones . . . there would be another scatter of rocks a bit further on"(25-5).

These were, of course, only the most preliminary forms of resistance; in fact the passage quoted is from a recollected speech O'Donnell made one day after Mass right outside the church itself. More important was the formation of organized branches of resistance, which O'Donnell explains in detail (25), and the actions taken by the collective whole once the organization had taken place — such as the official published declaration that no rents and no annuities were to be paid (39).

Of course, O'Donnell perforce discusses the political interplay between Sinn Fein, the I.R.A., and Fianna Fail — which resulted in no support of any kind for the Donegal agitators (34-37), who were left to go it courageously alone. As for O'Donnell's relations with the law-enforcing Free State government, the agitation was bothersome enough that O'Donnell found himself arrested and charged with communism by Paddy Hogan, Minister of Agriculture, in an attempt to discredit O'Donnell and his growing movement. He was then remanded in D Wing of Mountjoy prison — where he spent a good deal of his time in *The Gates Flew Open*. After his eventual acquittal and release, O'Donnell found himself harassed by virtually daily "nuisance" arrests, each lasting only a few hours but sometimes resulting in ruined activist plans.

One of the most engaging of O'Donnell's history lessons concerns the government's targeting of Croveigh, a Donegal townland, in December of 1927. This was truly serious business because now the government was going to go beyond the seizing of cattle.

With "decrees out against every holding" (60), the bailiffs were completing the return to nineteenth-century tactics — eviction and land sales. O'Donnell candidly reports his sense of political weakness at this juncture and declares his fear for the future. But encouragement was soon to come from the people themselves, as spontaneous acts of solidarity began to help fight the "war"— it is O'Donnell's term — for the agitators, such as the hiding of seizable cattle among the herds of solvent neighbors, after which they are sold and the money put into a "defence fund" to help those arrested or threatened with eviction. Eventually agitators began to be arrested for "debt" and jailed (64) —even an inspirational seventy-year-old man named Black James Duirnin. O'Donnell makes a brief but powerful statement on how hard prison is on these rural people — and it reminds us of O'Donnell's own first reactions to imprisonment in the initial chapter of *The Gates Flew Open*: "the walls seemed to press in against him and he just had to get out" (65). By degrees, O'Donnell's supporters began to lose heart and eventually he was asked to seek a sellout compromise with the government — with Paddy Hogan in particular. O'Donnell's interview with Hogan — one of the reasons O'Donnell was the sole person qualified to write this history — made it clear to him that the government, sensing O'Donnell's position of weakness, was completely unwilling to compromise (72). This unexpected turn of events permitted O'Donnell to return after his sincere efforts at compromise to what he knew how to do best: invent new resistance tactics. With the approval of his independent-minded committee of agitators, O'Donnell proposed that the majority of landholders pay what they owed and have only a few — who could withstand a jailing or the seizure of cattle — continue to resist in the same ways as before. As O'Donnell explains, this is not the end of the movement, despite appearances; it has merely been forced to go underground, as live coals can become hidden among the embers yet re-emerge after the ashes have been raked (76).

Perhaps O'Donnell's most intricate component history lesson occurs in the sixth chapter, where he first minutely explores the wording of the law of the 1920 Government of Ireland Act that required Ireland to pay annuities to the British; then explains how that law came to be annulled and how the Irish government adopted *voluntarily* the option to pay what was owed—a result of the treaty; and lastly, poses at some length the question. why should Irish farmers be obliged to pay off these "debts" instead of *all* Irishmen carrying a share of the load? (79-92). Here, as in the other places where O'Donnell — sometimes necessarily — begins to lecture, the flow of the narrative becomes still and the book loses its fascination. I say this not so much to fault O'Donnell as to say that he had little choice when writing a book so innately limited before the onslaught of time; that is, even by the time of its publication — 1963 — the vast majority of his readers would have little or no concept of the intricacies involved in understanding this historical episode — hence O'Donnell had no alternative but to write a highly personalized history.

The ultimate part of the historical retelling reveals the final and relatively sudden development of victory for O'Donnell and the agitators, who had seen the movement grow from Donegal to Galway and then all over rural Ireland. If we recall O'Donnell's short story, "War," wherein a group of farmers wonders if the distant Russo-Japanese war will affect them economically, then we can see a similar situation developing — albeit with a different outcome — regarding O'Donnell's movement; the world economic crisis of the early thirties hit Ireland, making the payment of annuities "an embarrassment" from an agriculturally impoverished country. This meant that "middle and even bigger farmers" involved themselves and the movement finally became "self-propelled" (112).

Next follows an anticlimactic lesson on the organization plan of the I.R.A., which seems only marginally necessary (114). More interesting is O'Donnell's detailing of peaceful I.R.A. involvement, after which we see the Cosgrave government voted out of office with what O'Donnell considered to be the tainted but nonetheless triumphant election of De Valera (131-32). The crisis was over, but the book's final words — exactly echoing its title — reveal O'Donnell contemplating the future: the day when Ireland's poor come to hold political power.

Fortunately, along the way, O'Donnell's creative imagination cannot help but commandeer his history book, albeit just a few pages at a time. Episodes such as his trial, for example, are highly engaging. So too is his direct approach in dealing with a greedy bailiff — manipulating and persuading the man in his own home; O'Donnell succeeds in convincing him to support the agitation —

yet still perform his office and continue to make his money. All he has to do is provide the names of those who bought seized cattle (32), so that later on agitators could visit the buyers and exert pressure on them. The interplay between the two men is realistic, yet also somewhat amusing as we see O'Donnell methodically win the argument and corner his victim until the bailiff has no choice but to comply. We sense O'Donnell persuasively smiling throughout the entire episode; threats play no part in it. In this same boldly direct manner — as boldly as he walked up to and out through the gates of Curragh camp — O'Donnell also deals with a man who has purchased seized cattle. The segment (40-47) is, in fact, an adventure in the repossession of seized cattle, culminating in O'Donnell's personal visit to the man's house. O'Donnell's tactic this time is to argue with the buyer in a friendly way until the man feels shame at having taken advantage of a neighbor's inability to pay arrears. This is the kind of pressure O'Donnell and his followers were able to apply once they had a list of names of those who had grabbed cattle; the importance of having the bailiff cooperate is underscored. Perhaps the most memorable of these kinds of passages concerns the saving of Jack Boyle's cattle, a part of the book we remember fondly along with O'Donnell not because of Jack Boyle — whom we never meet — but because of our introduction to Black James Duirnin, the seventy-year-old landholder we saw earlier who preferred to go to jail rather than give in to the British. In his discussion with Black James over what to do with Boyle's cattle when the bailiff comes, O'Donnell is touched by the old man's intensity and his instant formulation of a plan. Townland people will "make a place" for the cattle in their own byres at night, then draw carts across the road by day to avert any sudden raid by motor car (26). This is one of the best individual scenes we find in *There Will Be Another Day*, and O'Donnell betrays his conscious appreciation of such moments — not nearly as numerous as those in *Salud!* — when he declares, "that scene in Black James Duirnin's field of oats is one of my great 'stills' " (27).

O'Donnell's observations are not restricted to his townland neighbors or revolutionary comrades. In fact, his commentary on famous Irish leaders — perceptive as it may be — helps give the book even more the character of a history text. James Connolly, for example, is portrayed as a "Marxist-Socialist," and Cosgrave as virtually an incompetent. But O'Donnell spends the most effort in this respect on trying to explain De Valera. He points out a bitter irony about the man when he writes that "leadership was thrust on him by the firing parties that shot down the other chiefs of the Rising from around him" (13). As for De Valera's relationship to Ireland's middle and lower classes, O'Donnell observes that he "was numb, rather than hostile, to the working class struggle" (14).

Certainly of interest to the literary scholar — as they were in *The Gates Flew Open* and *Salud!* — are the brief references, scattered throughout, to his own efforts at literature. His thoughts on the land annuity agitation found an audience via *An Phoblacht*, a Republican newspaper with rural readership that O'Donnell edited between 1926 and 1934; as its editor, O'Donnell took the opportunity to air his views as well as to respond broadly to "official" government attacks on him and his movement. References to *The Gates Flew Open* are necessarily numerous, since *There Will Be Another Day* extends the action begun in the former book. O'Donnell makes mention of his escape (22), of his solitary confinement in Finner Camp (45), and of his continued acquaintances from that period (115). Much more significant are his references to *Adrigoole*. At one point O'Donnell declares that during his second round of imprisonment in Mountjoy the governor, named Faulkner, was an "understanding" man who let him send manuscripts out for typing, since he "was working on a novel at the time" (54). That novel he later identifies as *Adrigoole*, so it is clear that the novel was not written entirely free from the tension and interruption that were typical of the composing process of its predecessors. During this period of being daily arrested and harassed, he brought his work with him — requesting only tea while he wrote a chapter of the novel or composed an editorial for *An Phoblacht*. So once again, O'Donnell was forced to write creative literature — episodically — as a result of his political involvements. There can be little wonder that episodic literary art became his creative norm. It is, then, probably likely that the first part of *Adrigoole* was composed under these conditions, since it is the most engaging and seems most heartfelt. When the jailings stopped and O'Donnell was more free to set aside blocks of time in which to write, he probably became impatient because of his desire to lead the agitation and then wrote the fast-paced, far inferior second half of the novel. Most telling, however, is O'Donnell's admission that the novel's naturalism— with its concomitant inherent pessimism — did indeed stem from a period of personal crisis: "I often walked alone in the shadow of the hills. It was then that the sense of gloom and doom in my novel, *Adrigoole,* entered my mind. It disturbed me to recall how often I had billeted a considerable number of men in those homes in the Tan days. I was more aware now of the weakness of the economy. My eyes were sharper. I noticed how the heather ate its way into land that had fallen into feeble hands. It saddened me that mountains should renew their grip on fields that had been won from them by desperate, hopeful men" (22). Even these personal reminiscences carry the strong suggestion of the naturalistic dialectic, so one can see why O'Donnell's creative vision manifested itself the way it did at this point in his life: the naturalistic philosophy seemed borne out by life itself.

Wrack, O'Donnell's only play, is also naturalistic, and the lone reference to it in *There Will Be Another Day* supports this claim — which is not surprising since it was published relatively soon after *Adrigoole.* Of *Wrack* O'Donnell writes: "I intended it to be a glimpse of an island dying; the island I had in mind has since died" (129). Once again, life itself seems to bear out the naturalistic view of things. Also interesting is what O'Donnell goes on to tell us about how he passed the play on to Yeats, who, in "a friendly note," asked for a meeting, which O'Donnell requested be made secret in order to protect himself. Yeats went along with the idea and "made immediate and elaborate arrangements for [their] safe meeting." All of this, of course, led to the play's eventual production at the Abbey in 1932. O'Donnell's references to subsequent literary works are indirect and limited. Significantly, he makes no allusion at all to *The Knife;* by 1963 he was probably aware of that novel's serious defects. He does, however, make veiled mention of *On the Edge of the Stream,* his next fully creative work after *Wrack,* and *The Gates Flew Open.* In quoting from Liam Mellows's *Notes from Mountjoy Jail,* O'Donnell refers to the Catholic establishment's tendency — and long history — of siding politically against the people, especially the poor; instead the Church is too often allied with those who represent "commercial interests" and with "merchants" (10). Since this is exactly what happens in *On the Edge of the Stream* — perhaps most memorably in the Church-sponsored procession against the cooperative store — we can assume that O'Donnell had the novel in mind when he quoted from and commented on Mellows's *Notes*. Despite the passage of thirty years, O'Donnell's opinion remains unchanged and even the onset of old age has not mitigated his virtually lifelong indignation at how Ireland's poor farmers are treated. References to *The Big Windows* are even more indirect, usually detectable in anecdotes about country folk helping the movement; the same mores and established social norms can be found, indicating to what degree O'Donnell's fiction maintains its fidelity to actual life.

But there is in *There Will Be Another Day* one more indirect but far more substantial connection between it and *The Big Windows*, and that connection will serve to underscore what is probably the book's greatest merit: what we learn about O'Donnell personally and about his values in the broadest sense. In *The Big Windows*, one of the most touching episodes concerns Brigid's capacity to feel even for the socially ostracized and mentally disturbed Ann the Hill, whose psychological imbalance and frightening behavior can be ascribed to the huge tumor growing under her breast. Like his heroine, O'Donnell too had a great capacity to feel and experienced no qualms at all at accepting all people, regardless of how close to the borders of society they dwelt. Of a man O'Donnell met in Mountjoy prison, he writes:

> My pal among the prisoners was a shapeless, poor body, so twisted by his deformity that all he had to do was sit on the pavement and money fell from heaven into his cap; he told me he took as much as thirty pounds on the day of an All-Ireland final. Once I got my ears sharpened to his half-articulated words, I often hunkered beside him to probe into the strange world of the beggar. I came on him only once afterwards in the outside world. He was sprawled on the footpath beside his cap, his pushed-out eyes fixed on me, but he did not let on to know me until I squatted down beside him, and then his whole body danced and he beat the kerb with his hand. It was just that he was glad to see me. (54)

Indeed, physical deformity did not repel him; spiritual deformity — greed, betrayal, hypocrisy — most certainly always did. This, of course, points to his true view of religion as warm, helpful, and

sympathetic to society's least "respectable" individuals. The
Church, O'Donnell felt, should pay far more attention to beggars,
the diseased, and the hungry than to politically expedient middle-
class commercial interests.

Not surprisingly, O'Donnell did encounter some clerical interference, even in this peaceful campaign. At one point, O'Donnell
can declare that "the best way to keep priests out of politics is to
leave them out when they are out" (68). Concerning "the strange
attitude" of one bishop who supports the bailiffs against the agitators, O'Donnell says that no one should blame him for having an
opinion on the matter, but that O'Donnell and his compatriots
"had a right to warn him not to dress up as a bishop" (110) when he
spoke to the public about it. This man, identified as Dr. Fogarty,
Bishop of Killaloe, was assailed by O'Donnell particularly because
he had taken it upon himself to declare the non-payment of land
annuities a sin. After O'Donnell attacked him in a speech, Fogarty
took his petty revenge by withdrawing financial support from a
boy in Maynooth seminary, whose father had simply made no pro-
test over O'Donnell's speech. Of course, O'Donnell's injunction
against clerical interference never seemed to extend to that minority of the clergy who meddled in politics to the benefit of
O'Donnell's purposes. The seventh chapter, for example, which is
entirely dedicated to Father John Fahy's successful efforts at
spreading the agitation to Galway, best underscores O'Donnell's
double standard. Perhaps O'Donnell allowed himself such a standard because proportionately few priests followed their own lights
relative to the Catholic establishment's hard conservative line. At
any rate, Fahy's method — instead of organized resistance to annuities, having masses of individuals acting instead — met with his approval, since O'Donnell needed all the help he could get.
O'Donnell's tone is proud when he relates Fahy's adventures,
which included the priest's own eventual arrest and imprisonment. The other highly favorable portrait of a priest, in this case
one who remained neutral and uninvolved, is that of a certain Father Scanlan. O'Donnell's tendency always seems to be to favor re-
spectfully older priests — as is true of George Moore and Paul
Vincent Carroll, to name just two other Irish authors —because
they are fully formed as individuals and hence less prone to bursts
of sudden enthusiasm, and this holds true for Father Scanlon.

O'Donnell felt "great affection for the old man," in part because he had "put up with" a good deal from O'Donnell when O'Donnell was a schoolteacher in his parish(66).

The neighborly attitude we sense — toward Father Scanlan, in his dealings with the disabled beggar, and in his championing of the agitators in general — marks the idea of socialism that is perhaps uniquely O'Donnell's — a socialism based in rudimentary neighborliness. One of his early concerns in the campaign was "whether the recent strife had broken the pattern of neighbourliness among [Donegal farmers] that neighbours would not gather round the neighbour in trouble and save his cattle" (24). In another good case, we see the same impulse behind the "defence fund": "If a man lost a few head of cattle, a couple of his neighbours could put a value on them and the committee would then compensate him out of that fund. It was [our] belief that everybody on our side would willingly pay in one year's rent. The fund would last longer if we got hold of the seized cattle again and gave them back to the man who lost them or, if that was too dangerous, sell them and put that money back into the fund. . . . In time a very considerable defence fund was built up" (29). Although this suggestion originated in Nial Houston, a comrade in the agitation's early stages, O'Donnell's immediate embracing and support of the idea indicate how close it came to his own heart. Throughout his novels and other books, O'Donnell really never preaches his socialism outright, but the emphasis everywhere on community and neighborliness clearly indicates his position on the subject. It is obviously not doctrinaire.

O'Donnell's love for his people is the bedrock of all his philosophy and activism. Since he was "not known by appearance much, outside Dublin and Donegal," he was during his travels often able to join in provincial discussions that included negative comments "on this blackguard Peadar O'Donnell." Wisely, O'Donnell did a good deal of listening because he really cared what his countrymen thought; in fact, we get a significant additional insight here into his sense of humor when he wryly declares, "I always added to their store of knowledge and helped them abuse him" (49). To be privy to one of these discussions — wherein O'Donnell cursed out himself — would have been priceless.

Probably the most emotional moment of the campaign came not at its conclusion but during the early going, when his hero, seventy-year-old Black James Duirnin, was released from prison. When a "good-natured busybody of the parish with a weakness" for public displays collected twenty-five pounds from the community to present to Duirnin in compensation for his "martyrdom" (65), O'Donnell silently cursed what appeared to be the sullying of the old man's pure idealism with material contamination. But Duirnin's surprising response to the reward instead created a memorable moment for O'Donnell: Duirnin asked the man "to thank every person who had put a red penny into this fine gift and to say to them that he, himself, thanked them from his heart; it was clear that he was deeply moved. Up went the shaggy old head. 'Thank them and give them their money back. I went to jail for a principle. I could have paid the annuity and the arrears.' I just looked on, in a flood of tears, feeling a fool and, in my own way, rejoicing. I was there to see what I saw" (66).

This moment helped provide O'Donnell with the courage and inspiration to persevere despite the odds against him and his movement. The love between O'Donnell and his people formed the basis of what was actually a mutually expanding relationship: his dedication was an inspiration to them, just as their courage and devotion to the agitation motivated him. Cosgrave's government did not stand a chance.

Final Evaluation

Of the O'Donnell canon, Higgins has affirmed that its "achieve-ment is great,"[79] and Grattan Freyer asserts that "O'Donnell's books have a secure place in Anglo-Irish literature" because of their intrinsic appeal as works of art and because of their ability to portray "in a way no other author does certain aspects of regional culture and political history."[80] Richard Fallis finds him "one of the ablest of the Irish naturalists of his time," possessing an "im-pressive feel for County Donegal,"[81] while Norstedt, expressing a view no doubt held by the majority of sensitive readers who have enjoyed O'Donnell's work, feels that O'Donnell "does not deserve the neglect accorded him today" and that he is "one of the great characters on the Irish literary landscape of this century."[82]

Such accolades are warranted for a variety of reasons besides those incidentally mentioned above. Costello finds O'Donnell's rural portraits "moving,"[83] and indeed, if we recall the many times we have felt an intense connection with O'Donnell's characters, experiencing the intensity of their suffering and the beauty of their simple joys, we are likely to arrive at the same conclusion. Mercier is impressed with O'Donnell's "gift for surprisingly deli-cate psychological insight," although he sensibly admits that, gen-erally, O'Donnell has little gift for "physical description";[84] Mercier also notes that anything close to propaganda in O'Donnell's work is defeated by the author's "innate optimism,"[85] which suffuses all his fiction with the exception of *Adrigoole* and perhaps *Proud Island*.

His three greatest novels — *Islanders, On the Edge of the Stream,* and *The Big Windows* — are certainly thus distinguished, and although plot is not O'Donnell's strength, character almost always is — and it is character that we remember best: the admirable Mary and Charlie Doogan in *Islanders*, the suffering Nelly McFadden Joyce and endearing Donal Breslin in *On the Edge of the Stream*, and the powerful creation of Brigid Dugan Manus in *The Big Windows*. The everyday quality of their lives is better rendered, I believe, than by any other rural Irish novelist, past or present. *Islanders* and *The Big Windows* are undoubtedly classics, truly rural novels that rank alongside the more cosmopolitan-oriented work of Moore and Joyce and other serious rural novels such as the O'Flaherty epic, *Famine* (1937), and Figgis's *Children of Earth*.

On some levels, O'Donnell's novels and drama — and even some of the autobiographical vignettes — have a tendency to "blend" in the reader's memory. In part this is because the many characters are given basically the same names, albeit in different combinations. The major cause, however, is the lack of conventional plot, a point to which I have repeatedly alluded; the result is that we end by recalling one powerful scene after another from *various* works as much as we remember those works individually, if not more. This is not meant as negative criticism; indeed, we arrive at this synthesis willy-nilly and quite naturally, and the effect is of tremendous regional depth. That is, we come to know a *people* in an intimate way, and we care little, if at all, that such knowledge is derived from the reading of several novels.

That rich tapestry is all woven of the same cloth, with some parts more attractive than others, but with every part contributing significantly to the effect of the whole. No other Irish novelist of any real merit can make the same claim.

Notes

1. Ernest Boyd, *Ireland's Literary Renaissance* (New York: Knopf, 1922), p. 374.
2. Benedict Kiely, *Modern Irish Fiction* (Dublin: Golden Eagle, 1950), p. x.
3. Richard Fallis, *The Irish Renaissance* (Syracuse: Syracuse University Press, 1977), p. 133.
4. William J. McCormack, *Ascendancy and Tradition in Anglo-Irish Literary History from 1739-1939* (Oxford: Clarendon Press, 1985), p. 1.
5. On O'Flaherty see John Zneimer, *The Literary Vision of Liam O'Flaherty* (Syracuse: Syracuse University Press, 1970); Paul Doyle, *Liam O'Flaherty* (New York: Twayne, 1972); James O'Brien, *Liam O'Flaherty* (Lewisburg: Bucknell University Press, 1973); A. A. Kelly, *Liam O'Flaherty, The Storyteller* (New York: Barnes and Noble, 1977); and Patrick F. Sheeran, *The Novels of Liam O'Flaherty: A Study in Romantic Realism* (Atlantic Highlands, N.J.: Humanities Press, 1977). on James Stephens see Hilary Pyle, *James Stephens: His Works and an Account of his Life* (London: Routledge and Kegan Paul, 1965); Augustine Martin, *James Stephens: A Critical Study* (Dublin: Gill and Macmillan, 1977); Richard J. Finneran, *The Olympian and the Leprechaun: W. B. Yeats and James Stephens* (Dublin: Dolmen Press, 1978); and Patricia McFate, *The Writings of James Stephens* (New York: St. Martin's Press, 1979).
6. See Wayne Hall, "Esther Waters: An Irish Story," *Irish Renaissance Annual,* ed. Zack Bowen (Newark: University of Delaware Press, 1980): 137-156.
7. *Esther Waters* (London: Walter Scott, 1894), p. 163.
8. See for example Grattan Freyer, *Peadar O'Donnell* (Lewisburg: Bucknell University Press, 1973); Michael McInerney, *Peadar O'Donnell,*

Irish Social Rebel (Dublin: O'Brien Press, 1974); and Peter Costello, *The Heart Grown Brutal* (Dublin: Gill and Macmillan, 1977).

9.   See Freyer, pp. 103-17.

10. Freyer, p. 37.

11. Vivian Mercier, "Realism in Anglo-Irish Fiction 1916-1940" (Trinity College, Dublin: Doctoral Dissertation, 1943), p. 252.

12. Freyer, p. 38.

13. Grattan Freyer, " 'Big Windows' ": The Writings of Peadar O'Donnell," *Eire-Ireland* Volume 11, 1 (1976)p. 109.

14. *Storm* (Dublin: Talbot, 1925?), p. 7. All references are to this edition; page numbers will appear parenthetically in the text.

15. Mercier, p. 257.

16. Johann Norstedt, review of *The Knife* in *Irish Literary Supplement* Volume 2, 2 (1983)p. 20.

17. Freyer, *Peadar O'Donnell*, p. 40.

18. *Islanders* (London: G. P. Putnam's Sons, 1928), p. 150. All references are to this edition; page numbers will appear parenthetically in the text.

19. Freyer, "The Writings of Peadar O'Donnell," p. 110.

20. A. Norman Jeffares, *Anglo-Irish Literature* (Dublin: Macmillan, 1982), p. 232.

21. Freyer, *Peadar O'Donnell*, p. 42.

22. Mercier, p. 264.

23. *Adrigoole* (London: G. P. Putnam's Sons, 1929), p. 4. All references are to this edition; page numbers will appear parenthetically in the text.

24. Richard Fallis, *The Irish Renaissance* (Syracuse: Syracuse University Press, 1977), p. 206.

25. Freyer, *Peadar O'Donnell*, p. 46.

26. James Cahalan, *The Irish Novel: A Critical History* (Boston: Twayne, 1988), p. 192.

27. Freyer, "The Writings of Peadar O'Donnell," p. 110.

28. Freyer, *Peadar O'Donnell*, p. 48.

29. Fallis, p. 206.

30. Alan Warner, *A Guide to Anglo-Irish Literature* (New York: St. Martin's Press, 1981), p. 276.

31. Brenda O'Hanrahan, *Donegal Authors* (Dublin: Irish Academic Press, 1982), p. 206.

32. Fallis, p. 207.

3. Mercier, p. 270.

4. Mercier, p. 175.

5. Norstedt, p. 20.

6. Freyer, *Peadar O'Donnell*, p. 47.

7. *The Knife* (Dublin: Irish Humanities Centre, 1980), p. 169. All references are to this edition, which is more readily available than the first edition; page numbers will appear parenthetically in the text.

8. Norstedt, p. 20.

9. Fallis, p. 207.

0. Freyer, *Peadar O'Donnell*, p. 48.

1. Mercier, p. 274.

2. Norstedt, p. 20.

3. Norstedt, p. 20.

4. Mercier, p. 272.

5. Freyer, *Peadar O'Donnell*, p. 94.

6. Mercier, p. 282.

7. On the crosscurrents between sociology and literary criticism regarding O'Donnell's work, see Michael D. Higgins, "Liam O'Flaherty and Peadar O'Donnell—Images of Rural Community," *The Crane Bag* Volume 9, 1 (1985)pp. 41-48.

8. Mercier, p. 290.

9. Freyer, "The Writings of Peadar O'Donnell," p. 111.

0. *On the Edge of the Stream* (London: Jonathan Cape, 1934), p. 9. All references are to this edition; page numbers will appear parenthetically in the text.

1. Costello, p. 163.

2. See McInerney, p. 190.

3. Freyer, *Peadar O'Donnell*, p. 120.

4. Fallis, p. 206.

5. Dublin: O'Brien Press, 1985.

6. Freyer, *Peadar O'Donnell*, p. 124.

7. *The Big Windows* (London: Jonathan Cape, 1955), p. 37. All references are to this edition; page numbers will appear parenthetically in the text.

8. Freyer, *Peadar O'Donnell*, p. 123.

9. Freyer, *Peadar O'Donnell*, p. 124.

0. *Proud Island* (Dublin: O'Brien Press, 1975), p. 64. All references are to this edition; page numbers will appear parenthetically in the text.

61. *The Bell* 1, 1 (1940)pp. 60-62.

62. *The Bell* 1, 3 (1940)pp. 7-9

63. *The Bell* 15, 3 (1954)pp. 3-10

64. Freyer, *Peadar O'Donnell*, p. 104.

65. *Wrack* (London: Jonathan Cape, 1933), pp. 38-39. All references are to this edition; page numbers will appear parenthetically in the text.

66. Freyer, *Peadar O'Donnell*, p. 59.

67. *The Gates Flew Open* (London: Jonathan Cape, 1932), p. 139. All references are to this edition; page numbers will appear parenthetically in the text.

68. Freyer, *Peadar O'Donnell*, p. 56.

69. Freyer, *Peadar O'Donnell*, p. 57.

70. *Salud! An Irishman in Spain* (London: Methuen, 1937), p. 14. All references are to this edition; page numbers will appear parenthetically in the text.

71. Freyer, *Peadar O'Donnell*, p. 96.

72. Freyer, *Peadar O'Donnell*, p. 97.

73. McInerney, p. 186.

74. Costello, p. 292.

75. *There Will Be Another Day* (Dublin: Dolmen, 1963), p. 7. All references are to this edition; page numbers will appear parenthetically in the text.

76. Freyer, *Peadar O'Donnell*, p. 67.

77. Freyer, *Peadar O'Donnell*, p. 74.

78. Freyer provides a compact summary of these events. See *Peadar O'Donnell*, pp. 67-74.

79. Higgins, p. 45.

80. Freyer, "The Writings of Peadar O'Donnell," p. 106.

81. Fallis, pp. 206, 205.

82. Norstedt, p. 20.

83. Costello, p. 267.

84. Mercier, pp. 263, 264.

85. Mercier, p. 257.

Index